3人执裁基础

国际篮联裁判员手册

中国篮球协会 审定

北京体育大学出版社

策划编辑：曾　莉
责任编辑：曾　莉　　李　涛
责任校对：吴海燕　　王泓滢
版式设计：高文函

图书在版编目（CIP）数据

国际篮联裁判员手册 . 3 人执裁基础 / 中国篮球协会审定 . -- 北京：北京体育大学出版社，2021.9（2024.4 重印）
ISBN 978-7-5644-3494-6

Ⅰ . ①国… Ⅱ . ①中… Ⅲ . ①篮球运动—裁判法—手册 Ⅳ . ① G841.4-62

中国版本图书馆 CIP 数据核字（2021）第 189989 号

国际篮联裁判员手册：3 人执裁基础　　中国篮球协会　审定

出版发行：北京体育大学出版社
地　　址：北京市海淀区农大南路 1 号院 2 号楼 2 层办公 B-212
邮　　编：100084
网　　址：http: //cbs.bsu.edu.cn
发 行 部：010-62989320
邮 购 部：北京体育大学出版社读者服务部 010-62989432
印　　刷：河北盛世彩捷印刷有限公司
开　　本：880mm × 1230mm　　1/32
成品尺寸：145mm × 210mm
印　　张：3.75
字　　数：104 千字
版　　次：2021 年 11 月第 1 版
印　　次：2024 年 4 月第 3 次印刷
定　　价：28.00 元

出版说明

- 《国际篮联裁判员手册：3 人执裁基础》由中国篮球协会依照国际篮球联合会（简称“国际篮联”）发布的 FIBA Referees Manual 翻译和修订。今后所有正式国际篮球比赛和国内篮球比赛，以及各类篮球裁判员晋级考试，均按最新《篮球规则》及《国际篮联裁判员手册》执行。

- 《国际篮联裁判员手册：3 人执裁基础》的翻译和编订力求忠实于原文。如在理解和执行过程中出现争议，以国际篮联官方语言英文版为准。翻译和审校工作可能存在疏漏之处，欢迎广大读者提出意见和建议，以便我们及时修订和完善。

- 整本《国际篮联裁判员手册：3 人执裁基础》中所有提到的教练员、运动员、技术官员等都是男性，同样也适用于女性。必须强调，这样写只是为了实用的缘故。

FOREWORD

Basketball, as a game, is progressing in skill and speed every day. It is a natural environmental development process that takes place unconditionally and it is called evolution. The game and more so refereeing has completely changed from 10 years ago. Presently, top level refereeing is improving at least at the same speed as the game itself and higher standards of performance are expected every year. The pace of change has necessitated the adoption of a motto: "What was considered exceptionally good yesterday, is considered standard quality today and below average quality tomorrow".

This FIBA Basic 3 Person Officiating Manual provides the foundational mechanical steps required for successful basketball refereeing.

This manual complements other FIBA technical manuals and supporting material, namely "Improve Your..." series (for example 'Improve Your... Rotation'). These brief guides provide more insight and details on how to work with the content mentioned in this manual.

In the case of a discrepancy between any guidelines in the Manual and the Official Basketball Rules (OBR) and/or the Official Basketball Rules Interpretations (OBRI), the latter (OBR and OBRI) will prevail.

前　言

篮球作为一项运动，在技术和速度方面每天都在进步，它是一种自然发展过程，无条件发生，被称为演变。比赛本身以及执裁方式与10 年前完全不同。目前，顶级的执裁方式的进展速度快于篮球比赛本身，并且每年都有更高的裁判规范标准。目前的发展速度使我们树立了一个座右铭："过去被视为极好的标准，在当前是普通标准，到了将来会低于平均标准。"

《国际篮联裁判员手册：3 人执裁基础》提供了成功执裁所必须的裁判法步骤。

本手册是对其他国际篮联技术手册和辅助资料的补充，比如"提高你的……"系列（例如"提高你的……轮转"）。这些简要的指导文件都在本手册的基础上提供给裁判员更多执裁工作中的理念和细节。

如果本手册的任何指导方针与官方《篮球规则》和/或官方《篮球规则解释》有不一致之处，以后者（官方《篮球规则》和/或官方《篮球规则解释》）为准。

TABLE OF CONTENTS

CHAPTER 1

CHAPTER 2

目录

第 1 章

第 2 章

CHAPTER 3

第3章

国际篮联裁判员手册
3 人执裁基础
（英文版）

第1章

INTRODUCTION & GENERAL

导论与通则

CHAPTER 1

1. INTRODUCTION & GENERAL

1.1 BASKETBALL OFFICIATING

Generally, sports officiating is challenging and more so in the game of basketball – especially where ten athletic players are moving fast in a restricted area. Naturally the game has changed and the court has actually become larger, not in actual court size but in the playing and refereeing sense. Play situations are spread all over the court with every player able to play in almost every position. Naturally this sets a new requirement for basketball refereeing. It is good to remember that improving daily should not be considered as actual progress but rather is only designed to keep pace with the game's development – this is called evolution and this will occur regardless if we want it or not.

Sometimes there is a tendency to define basketball officiating as a very complex combination of various skills. It is true it requires many abilities by the referee, but the bottom line is that all these skills aim to achieve one thing - being ready to referee the play or handle situations that may arise during the game.

Refereeing is:

Anticipate what will happen — Active mind-set
Understand what is happening — Basketball knowledge
React properly for what has happened — Mental Image Training

1.2 IMAGE OF AN ELITE BASKETBALL REFEREE

FIBA has one golden rule when it comes to prioritising referee training for FIBA games - Game Control. The intent is to ensure a smooth running and dynamic game where players are able to showcase their basketball skills. This is the image FIBA is looking for. The two or three appointed referees are the ones who are responsible for this game control.

第 1 章

1. 导论与通则

1.1 篮球比赛执裁

一般而言，执裁体育比赛是十分具有挑战性的，在篮球比赛中更是如此——特别是当 10 名运动员在有限的空间范围内快速移动时。自然而然地，比赛就发生了很多变化，比赛场地实际上变大了。这不是篮球场的实际大小发生变化，而是对比赛和执裁的意义上而言的。对抗的情况遍布全场，每个队员几乎都能在任何位置上进行比赛。自然，这为篮球裁判的工作提出了新的要求。最好记住，日常业务改进和提高难以被称为业务能力的进步，而只是作为跟上篮球运动发展节奏的必备条件。这就是所谓的进步，并且无论我们同意与否，都会发生这种改变。

有这样一种趋势，将执裁篮球比赛定义为一项包含多种不同复杂技能的综合体。确实，它需要裁判员具备多项能力。但底线是，所有技能都旨在达成一个目标，准备好执裁比赛或处理好比赛中可能出现的情况。

执裁是：

预测场上将要发生什么——动态思维
理解场上正在发生什么——篮球知识
恰当反映已经发生什么——心理训练

1.2 精英篮球裁判员的形象

在国际篮联的裁判员培训中心有一项优先开展的培训，也就是国际篮联的黄金法则——比赛控制。目的是确保比赛能够流畅顺利且具有活力地进行，以便让运动员能够充分展示自己的篮球技能，这是国际篮联希望发生的情况。归根结底，裁判员要对比赛负责。

It is good to define and remember that game control is different to game management. Ultimately, it is the Referees that are in charge of the game. They define what is allowed and what is not – nobody else.

Having said that, it is equally important that referees look and act like they are in charge. Referees should give a non-verbal message that they are ready and able to make decisions. The core function of refereeing is decision making. Referees need to feel comfortable in making decisions without hesitation in the decision making process. Of course, the correctness of these decisions can be analysed after the event and so referees must demonstrate confidence and trust or at the very least present so that others view them this way (perception).

Therefore, FIBA has added the topic of "court presence" to its training program. It includes mental training with an "I am in charge" concept. This will be combined with a physical training plan to create an image of a strong and athletic body, fitting into the image of professionalism and promoting game control.

"Controlling is an attitude"

记住控制比赛和管理比赛是不同的。最终，裁判员要对比赛负责——绝不是其他人。他们定义什么是允许的，什么是不被允许的。

行文至此，裁判员的形象和举止也是同样重要的。裁判员应当以非语言的信号来表现出自己已经做好准备并且能够很好地执裁比赛。执裁的核心要义是决策。裁判员需要在决策过程中毫不犹豫地做出决定。当然，这些决定的正确与否可以在赛后进行分析总结。因此，裁判员必须表现出自信和信任，或者至少是在当下，让其他人看起来他们是这样的。

因此，国际篮联在训练计划中增加了“赛场仪容仪表”的课题。它包含了以“我在执裁”为核心的心理表象训练内容。这将与体能训练计划相结合，打造一个强壮的运动型身体形象，以适应专业形象并提升对比赛的控制。

“控制是一种态度”

第2章

BASIC THREE PERSON OFFICIATING

3人执裁基础

CHAPTER 2

2. BASIC THREE PERSON OFFICIATING

2.1 INTRODUCTION

Three Person Officiating (3PO) is a great tool to implement correct IOT principles and to provide more time to actually process the play analytically (start-middle-end of the play) before making a decision. The analyses show that correct "no calls" are higher with 3PO than 2PO, and first illegal actions are called rather than reactions.

The key to successful 3PO is one simple word: trust. You must trust your partners. Only then can you concentrate on your primary area of coverage, and not have to worry about what is going on in your partner's area.

2.2 SYMBOLS USED

SYMBOL	EXPLANATION
	Trail referee or "T", in green colour on diagrams. Lead referee or "L", in blue colour on diagrams. Centre referee or "C", in red colour on diagrams. The base of the triangle represents the facing direction of the referee.
	Previous positions of Trail, Lead and Centre. Same principle (grey=previous) is applied to all symbols (ball, players etc.)
	Crew Chief (CC), Umpire 1 (U1), Umpire 2 (U2)
	Direction of the play
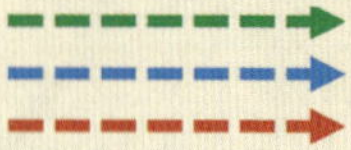	Direction of the Trail (green), Lead (blue) and Centre (red) referee

第 2 章

2. 3 人执裁基础

2.1 引言

3 人执裁是一种很好的正确运用个人执裁技术原则的方法，而且在做出决定前为准确分析处理比赛（动作开始—发展—结束的全过程）提供了更多时间。分析表明，3 人执裁中正确的“不宣判”情况要比 2 人执裁更多，并且对于非法的第一动作要做出宣判而不只是反应。

成功的 3 人执裁关键要点是：信任。你必须相信你的同伴。只有这样，你才能够集中注意力于你的主要责任区，而不会去关心你同伴的责任区里发生了什么。

2.2 使用的符号

符号	注释
	追踪裁判或“T”，图示为绿色 前导裁判或“L”，图示为蓝色 中央裁判或“C”，图示为红色 三角形的底边代表裁判员面向的方向
	灰色代表追踪裁判、前导裁判和中央裁判 相同的准则（灰色的 = 先前的）适用于所有的符号（包括球、队员等）
	主裁判（CC），第一副裁判（U1），第二副裁判（U2）
	比赛方向
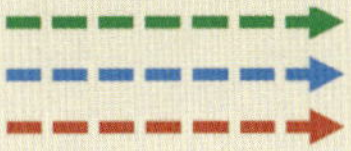	追踪裁判（绿色）、前导裁判（蓝色）和中央裁判（红色）的移动方向

SYMBOL	EXPLANATION
	Referee blowing the whistle
	Action Spot - Foul Called
	Coverage area
	Reporting referee indicated by the frame colour (T=green, L=blue, C=red)
A1 B1	Player A1 (offensive player), B1 (defensive player)
	Dribble

符号	注释
	裁判员鸣哨
	动作发生地点——宣判犯规
	视野覆盖区域
	边框的颜色表示正在报告的裁判员 （T= 绿色，L= 蓝色，C= 红色）
A1 B1	队员 A1（进攻队员），B1（防守队员）
	运球

2.3 GENERAL COURT POSITIONS

Target: Understand the basic court positions of Trail, Lead and Centre in 3PO, and positions before the game and during the time-outs.

Let's start with some key terms regarding the court positions.

TERM	EXPLANATION
Strong side –refereeing (SSR)	Side of the court where the Lead & Trail referees are located (in 3PO).
Weak side – refereeing (WSR)	Side of the court where the Centre referee is located (in 3PO).
Ball-side (BS)	This refers to the position of the ball. When the playing court is divided by an imaginary line extending from basket to basket, the side of the playing court on which the ball is located is called the "ball-side".
Help side (HSB)	The half of the front court opposite to where the ball is located.
Table side (TS)	This refers to the side of the playing court which is closest to the scorer's table.
Opposite side (OPS)	This refers to the side of the playing court which is furthest away from the scorer's table.
Trail (T)	The Trail is the referee who is positioned approximately at the edge of the team bench area nearer to the centre line and on the same side as the L (always strong side) and who stands behind the play.
Lead (L)	The Lead is the referee who is positioned at the endline. The Lead should be always on the ball-side as much of possible (strong side).
Centre (C)	The Centre is the referee who is positioned on the opposite side of the frontcourt from the L (usually opposite ball-side) at the free-throw line extended (set-up position). Depending on the location of the ball, C may be on either side of the frontcourt. Standard working area for C is on the court.

2.3 通常的场上位置

目标：理解 3 人执裁中追踪裁判、前导裁判和中央裁判基本的场上位置，以及比赛开始前和暂停期间的位置。

先依据场上的位置了解一些重要的术语。

术语	注释
强侧 – 执裁（SSR）	前导裁判与追踪裁判所在一侧的场地（3 人执裁时）
弱侧 – 执裁（WSR）	中央裁判所在一侧的场地（3 人执裁时）
球侧（BS）	此术语涉及球的位置。在两个球篮间用一条假想的线将球场划分为两部分，球所在的场地一侧为“球侧”
协助侧（HSB）	球所在前场场地的对面一侧
记录台侧（TS）	指靠近记录台的场地一侧
对侧（OPS）	指远离记录台的场地一侧
追踪裁判（T）	追踪裁判是大约落位于靠近中线的球队席区域边界的裁判员，同时与 L 在同一侧（强侧），并且位于比赛的后方
前导裁判（L）	前导裁判是落位于端线的裁判员。他的位置应始终尽最大可能地位于球侧（强侧）
中央裁判（C）	中央裁判是落位于 L 所在前场的对侧的裁判员（通常在球侧对面），在（初始位置）罚球线延长线。根据球的位置，C 可以位于前场的任意一侧。C 的标准工作区域在场地内

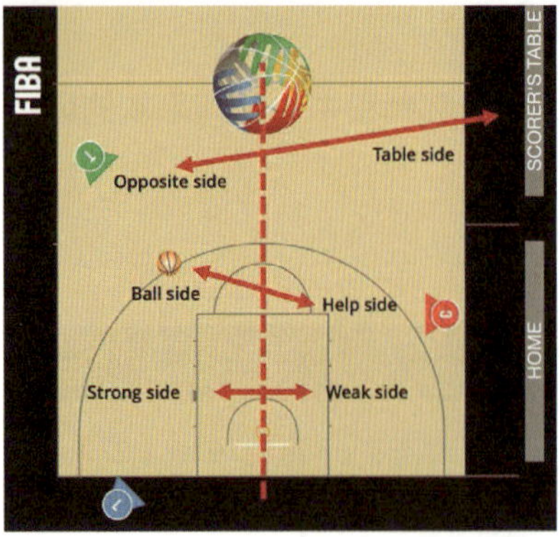

Diagram 1:
Trail, Lead, Centre, Strong side, Weak side, Ball side,Help side, Table side and Opposite side.

The whole idea of 3PO is based on the concept that two referees (T & L) are on ball side as much as possible. This gives them at least two different angles on ball side play situations and analyses has demonstrated that this leads to higher decision making accuracy. To achieve this during the game the referees need to adjust their triangle by rotating (see "*2.8 Rotation*").

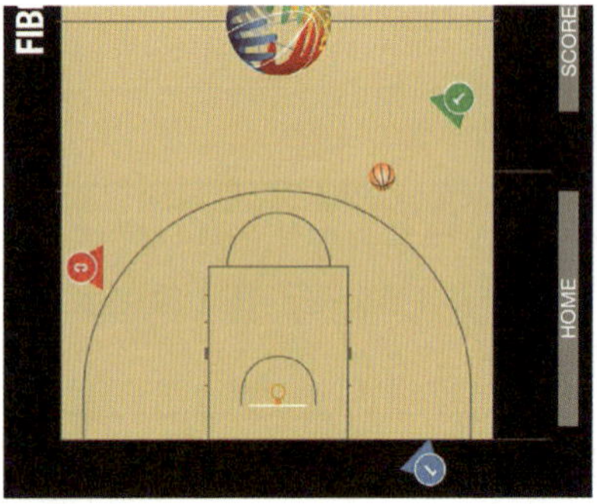

Diagram 2:
Front court basic positions for Trail, Lead and Centre when the L is located on the table-side.

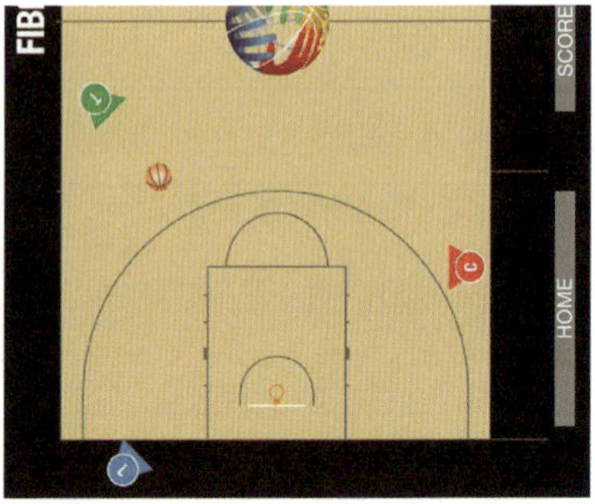

Diagram 3:
Front court basic positions for Trail, Lead and Centre when the L is located on opposite-side.

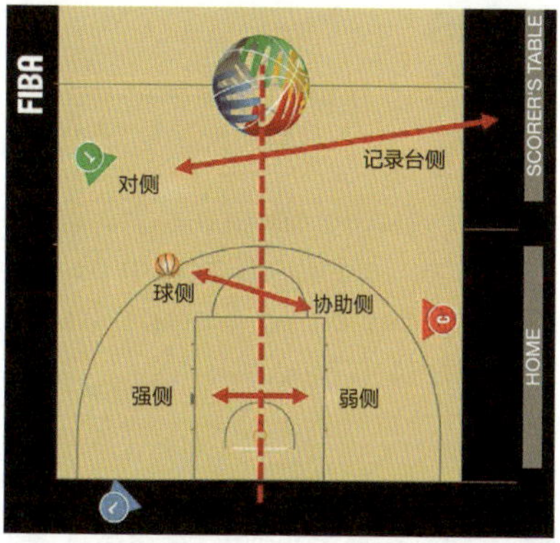

图 1：
追踪裁判（T）、前导裁判（L）、中央裁判（C）、强侧、弱侧、球侧、协助侧、记录台侧、对侧

3 人执裁的整体理念是将两名裁判员（T & L）尽可能保持在球侧。这利于裁判员观察球侧的比赛情况。通过分析已经表明，这可以有效提高执裁的准确性。为了在比赛中实现这一目标，裁判员需要不断地通过轮转来调整其三人的三角形位置。（见“2.8 轮转”）

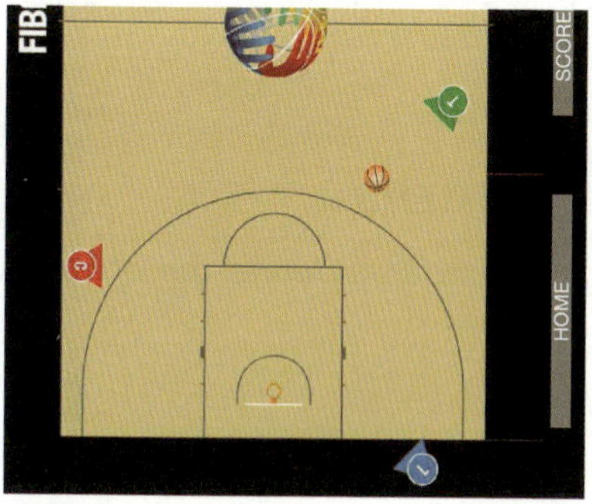

图 2：
当 L 在记录台同侧时，前场的追踪裁判、前导裁判和中央裁判的初始位置

图 3：
当 L 落位于对侧时，前场的追踪裁判、前导裁判和中央裁判的初始位置

2.4 PRE-GAME / HALF-TIME POSITIONS

The standard positioning before the game and during the half-time is described in Diagram 4.

If the referees are warming-up properly, one referee observes the court while the other two warm-up on the outside of the sideline (Diagram 5). The referees should rotate into different positions in order to have a proper warm-up and to observe the teams. More on this subject in "Improve Your... Game Warm Up & Streching" publication.

Diagram 4:
Standard pre-game position.

Diagram 5:
Optional pre-game position when two referees can warm-up all the time.

2.5 JUMP BALL & START OF THE QUARTERS

Target: To identify and understand the procedures during the opening jump ball and start of the quarters.

The position of the referees during the opening jump-ball:

1. The Crew Chief (CC) is responsible for tossing the jump ball from a position facing the scorer's table.
2. The umpires take positions on the opposite sidelines. U1 is table-side close to midcourt line and U2 is opposite side, near the edge of the team bench area.
3. U1 responsibilities:
    a. Calling for a re-jump on a poor toss or a jumper violation.

2.4 赛前和半时的位置

图 4 展示了比赛前和半场时裁判员的标准位置。

如果裁判员要进行适当的热身，应当留一名裁判员观察场上情况，另外两名裁判员在边线外进行热身（图 5）。裁判员可以交替热身，并保持观察球队情况。详细内容见已发布的“改进你的……赛前热身与拉伸”。

图 4：
比赛前裁判员标准站位

图 5：
赛前两名裁判员热身时的可选位置

2.5 跳球和每节的开始

目标：确认和理解跳球和每节比赛开始的程序。

开场跳球时裁判员的位置：

1. 主裁判（CC）负责从面对记录台的位置跳球抛球。
2. 两名副裁判站在相对的两条边线位置。U1 站在记录台侧靠近中场位置的边线，U2 站在对侧的球队席界线的位置。
3. U1 的责任：

   a. 在抛球不好时宣判重新跳球或跳球队员违例。

b. Giving the time-in signal to start the game clock when ball is legally tapped.

4. U2 responsibility: observing the eight (8) non-jumpers for possible violations and fouls.

Diagram 6:
The Crew Chief administers the toss and U1 is located close to midcourt line to observe possible poor toss and violations by jumpers, U2 is located opposite site observing the possible violations by non-jumpers.

Jump ball – play goes to Crew Chief's left

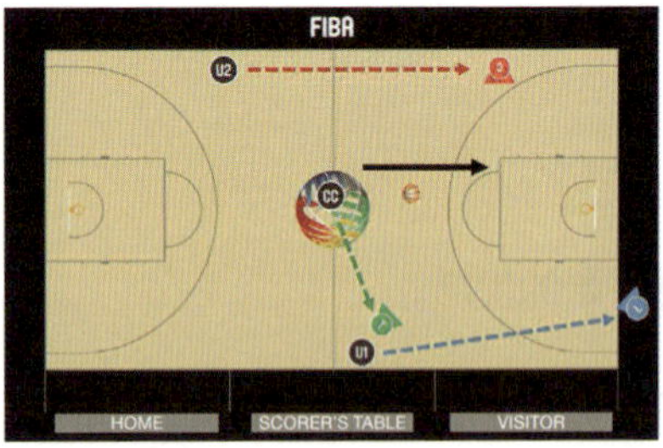

Diagram 7:
1) U1 becomes L, 2) U2 becomes C, 3) The Crew Chief moves to the sideline where was U1 and become T.

Jump ball – play goes to Crew Chief's right

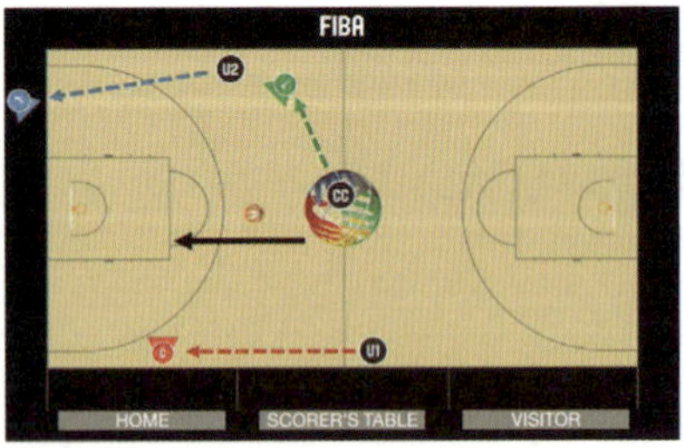

Diagram 8:
1) U2 becomes L, 2) U1 becomes C, 3) The Crew Chief (CC) moves to the sideline where was U2 and become T.

b. 当球被合法拍击时，做出开动比赛计时钟的手势。

4. U2 的责任：观察其他 8 名非跳球队员，是否出现违例和犯规。

图 6：
主裁判执行抛球，U1 位于靠近中线的位置观察可能存在的抛球失误或跳球队员违例，U2 位于场地对侧观察非跳球队员可能出现的违例

跳球后比赛向主裁判左侧发展

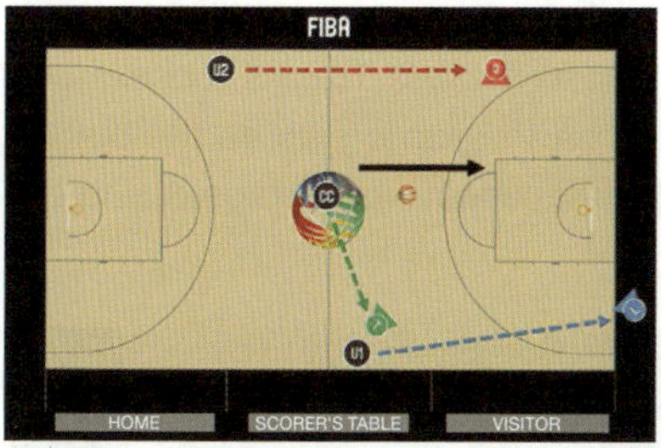

图 7：
1）U1变成L，2）U2变成C，3）主裁判（CC）移动到之前U1的边线位置变成T

跳球后比赛向主裁判右侧发展

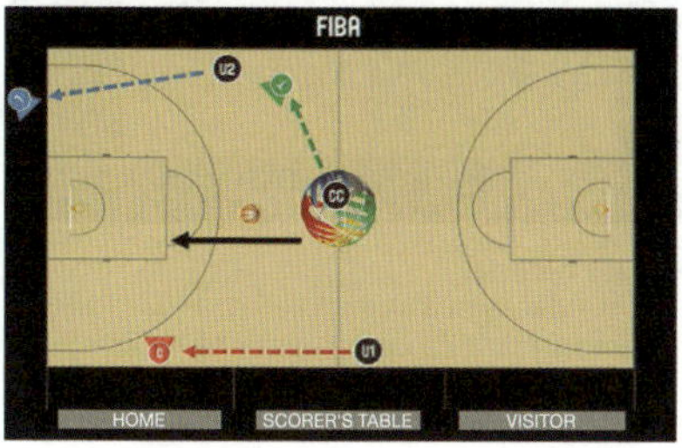

图 8：
1）U2变成L，2）U1变成C，3）主裁判（CC）移动到之前U2的边线位置变成T

Start of the 2nd, 3rd & 4th quarter and overtime:

The positioning of the referees is 1) The Crew Chief (CC) administers the throw-in at midcourt and becomes T 2) U1/U2 position themselves in L position opposite-side and in C position table-side.

Diagram 9:
The Crew Chief will always be the administering referee for the throw-in opposite-side to start the quarters. U1 and U2 will place themselves either in L or C position.

2.6 COURT COVERAGE

Target: To identify and understand the basic coverage in the frontcourt.

The basic principle of 3PO is that each referee has responsibility for their own area. Trust with partners has to be built to achieve this. As a basic rule, however, it is critical to have two referees on the same side as the ball as much as possible in order to make sure there is effective coverage during act of shooting situations.

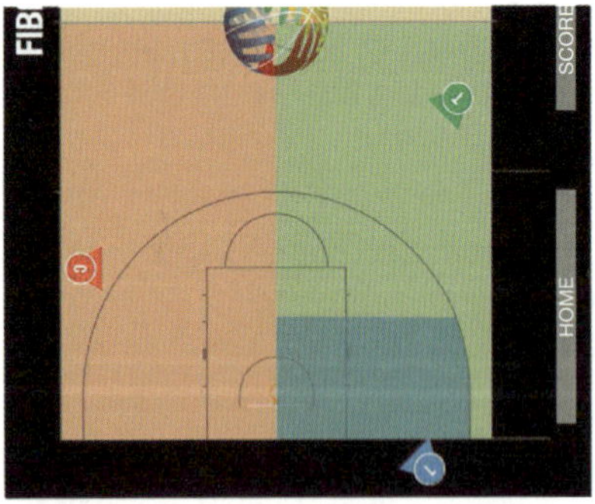

Diagram 10:
Court coverage in principle by all T, L and C when the L is located on the table-side.

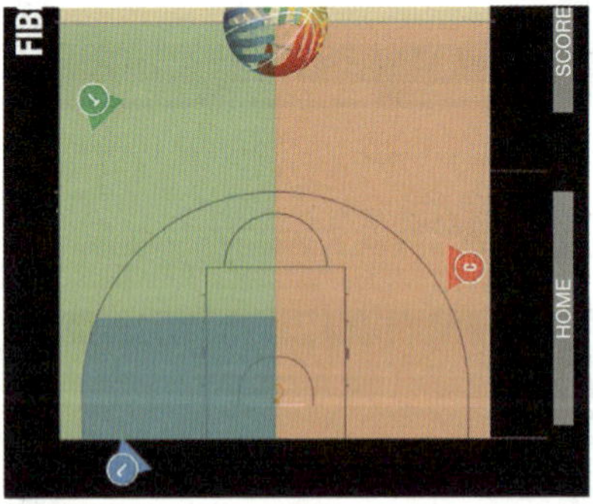

Diagram 11:
Court coverage in principle by all T, L and C when the L is located on opposite-side.

第 2 节、第 3 节、第 4 节和决胜期比赛的开始：

裁判员的站位是：1）主裁判（CC）在中线处管理掷球入界并成为 T；2）U1/U2 分别落位于对侧 L 和记录台侧 C 的位置。

图 9：
主裁判总是成为在每节比赛开始时管理对侧掷球入界的裁判员。U1 和 U2 可以落位于任一 L 或 C 的位置

2.6 场上的区域分工

目标：区分和理解在前场的基本区域分工。

3 人执裁的基本原则是每名裁判员要对自己的区域负责。通过建立同伴之间的信任来实现这一原则。然而作为基本的规则，必须要尽可能保持球侧有两名裁判员，来确保在投篮动作发生时有效的视野覆盖。

图 10：
当 L 位于记录台侧时，T、L 和 C 的责任区域

图 11：
当 L 位于对侧时，T、L 和 C 的责任区域

In the diagrams above, the Lead has the smallest area of coverage by size, but the analyses clearly indicate that the Lead still makes about 50-60% of all foul calls in the game. This is the result of the so called “action area” (also known as “bus-station”) which is the post on the ball-side. In other words, most of the plays end up in the action area and if Lead is on ball-side, as Lead should be, they have the best angle to cover any play in the action area. This is why it is critical to have two referees (T&L = strong side) on ball side as much as possible.

2.7 BASIC POSITIONING

2.7.1 LEAD POSITION

Target: To identify proper working area and coverage in the Lead positon.

Lead works on the baseline on a 45° angle facing the basket. Position should be not more than 1 metre from the baseline and normally outside the paint. The Lead’s working area is from three-point line to the edge of the backboard.

The normal set-up point for Lead is between the lane line of the key, and the three-point line. The Lead should move on the baseline according to the movement of the ball, ensuring they have position on the edge of the play. The Lead should work off-the court.

The Lead should normally make all violation/foul calls on the strong side of the court below free-throw line. Studies have proved that when the Lead makes calls on the weak side (other side of the court), especially on a drive (high contact), the decisions are incorrect, and in many cases, fantasy calls occur with guessing (foul called where contact was legal or no contact at all). This type of call is called “Lead cross call” and should not happen. The Lead must trust that the Centre will make the call if there is illegal contact (trusting Lead & active Centre). On weak side drives Lead may call low and front swipes and illegal hand contacts from Lead´s side and which Centre is unable to see. Lead must have an open angle to make the call.

在上图的区域中，尽管前导裁判覆盖最小的区域，但是分析表明他仍然吹罚了 50%~60% 的犯规。这个区域被称作“动作区域（或站台区）”，它主要存在于球侧。换言之，大量比赛片段发生在该区域，那么当前导裁判位于此处时，他将拥有最好的角度去观察该区域的比赛。这也是为什么球侧要尽可能有两名裁判员（T & L= 强侧）非常重要的原因。

2.7 基础位置

2.7.1 前导裁判的位置

目标：明确前导裁判的执裁位置和覆盖区域。

前导裁判在端线面对球篮，呈 45° 站位。站位地点不应该远离端线超过 1 米，并且应当在“限制区”的外侧。前导裁判的移动范围应当在 3 分线到篮板边缘之间。

前导裁判一般的初始位置位于限制区边界线与 3 分线之间。前导裁判应根据球的发展沿着端线移动，确保位于比赛边缘的位置。前导裁判应在场地外执裁。

前导裁判应当判罚出位于强侧罚球线以下的所有违例和犯规。研究证明，当前导裁判吹罚弱侧时（场地的另一侧），尤其是针对持球突破（高位的接触），决定一般都是错的，在很多案例中，都是伴随着猜测的猜判，吹罚的犯规都是合法接触或根本没有接触，这被称为“前导裁判的跨区交叉宣判”。前导裁判必须相信，如果那些位置发生非法接触，中央裁判将会做出判罚（信任的前导裁判和积极的中央裁判）。对于弱侧的突破，前导裁判可以对低位的、前侧的击打以及前导裁判一侧的非法手部接触进行判罚，而这些动作，中央裁判是无法看到的。前导裁判必须有很好的开角来做出判罚。

Diagram 12:
Lead working area is between 3 point line and edge of the board. To find out if you have the correct position is to check that you will see the front of the rim.

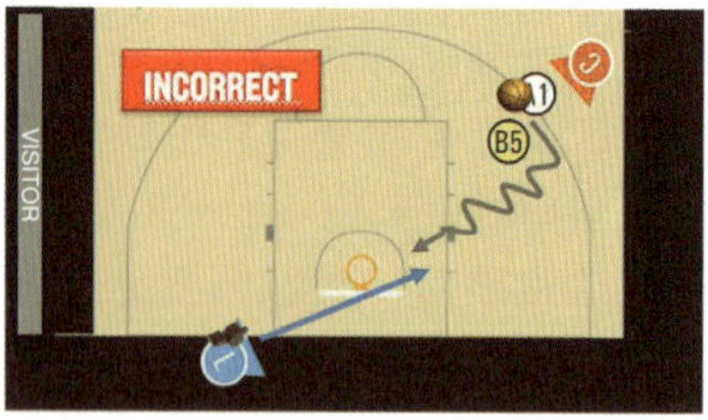

Diagram 13:
Lead must trust to the Centre who has to be active and ready cover his/her primary. The diagram demonstrates the "cross call" by Lead what is incorrect.

When ball comes to the strong side post (Lead's side) lead should prepare for a possible drive to the basket by taking few steps wider. This is called "Lead cross step". This allows Lead to see a possible drive to the basket, identify the possible help defence from the weak side, and implement the same "Distance & Stationary" principle as in transition.

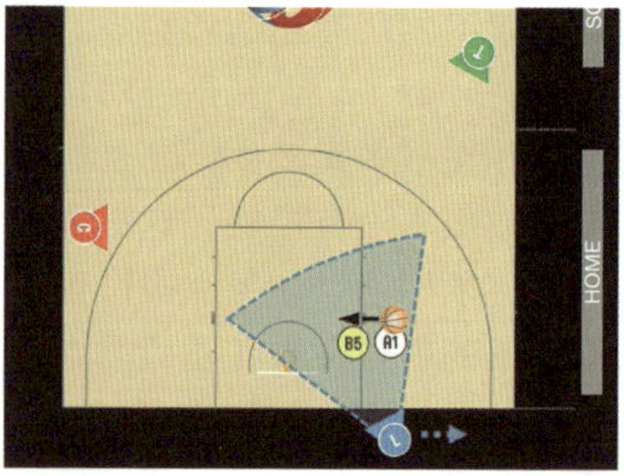

Diagram 14:
When ball comes to the strong side low post, Lead prepares for the next play and by taking cross steps to have wider angle covering the next possible play.

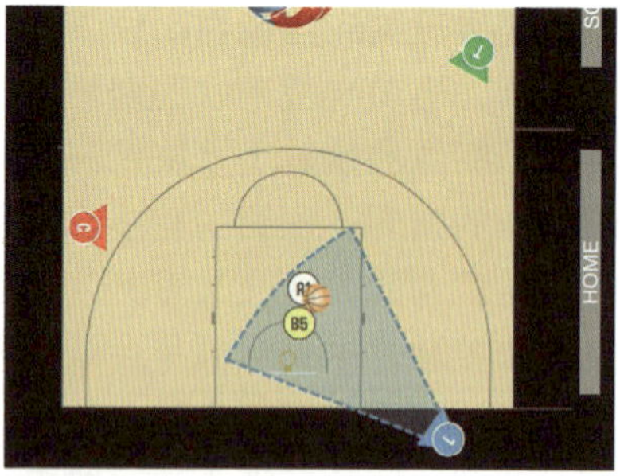

Diagram 15:
L has taken the cross steps and turned slightly towards the basket. This new angle allows to referee the defence in the drive and prepare for the help defense.

图 12：
前导裁判的工作区域位于 3 分线和篮板边缘之间。确认是否位于正确的位置可观察是否能看到篮圈前沿

图 13：
前导裁判必须信任中央裁判的活跃性和覆盖首要责任区的准备。图例展示了前导裁判错误的“越区判罚”

当来球到强侧中锋位置（前导裁判一侧）时，前导裁判应准备通过向外侧移动几步来看清可能的突破上篮。这被称作“前导裁判的交叉步”。这能帮助前导裁判观察可能的突破上篮，看清可能的来自弱侧的协防，在攻防转换中要用同样的“距离和静止”原则。

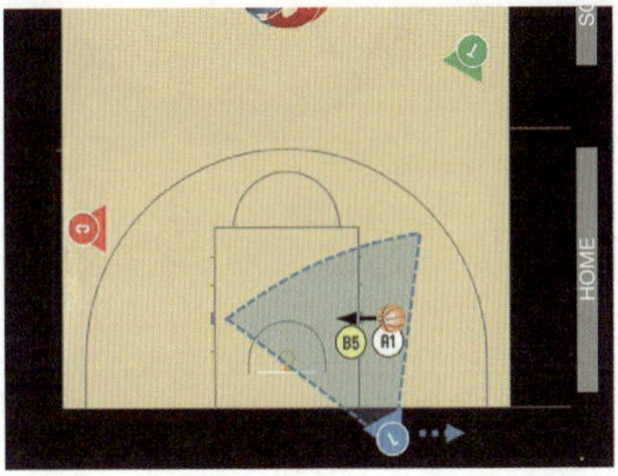

图 14：
当球位于强侧低位时，前导裁判应当为下一个动作做好准备并通过一个交叉步为下一个可能的动作获取更宽的视角

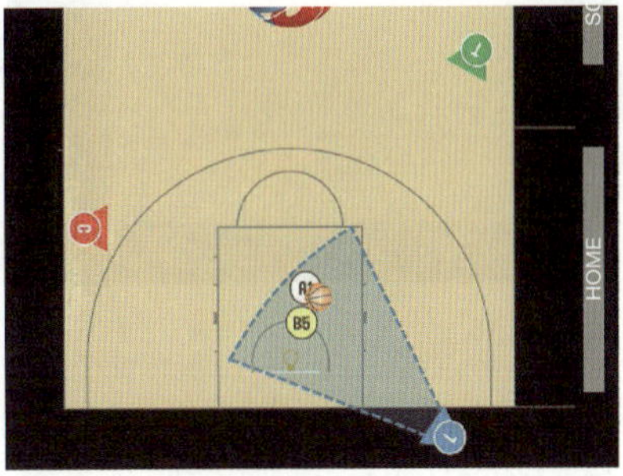

图 15：
L 做了一个交叉步和向球篮的轻微移动，新的视角使得裁判可以执裁突破中的防守并为协防做好准备

2.7.2 TRAIL POSITION

Target: To identify proper working area and coverage in the Trail position.

Trail working area is between team bench area line and centre line. The Trail should be able to control a wide area if they are keeping a proper distance from the players with an active mind-set to analyse the next movements of the players. Trail normally works on the court.

When the ball moves closer to the Trail's sideline, Trail should move further into the court to maintain the open angle. Whenever a dribbler is positioned in front of Trail, the Trail should be assessing which direction the dribbler will move next. Whenever a player moves in one direction, the Trail should move to the other direction - this is called "Trail Cross Step". When the play is over, the Trail should return closer to the sideline in the standard working position.

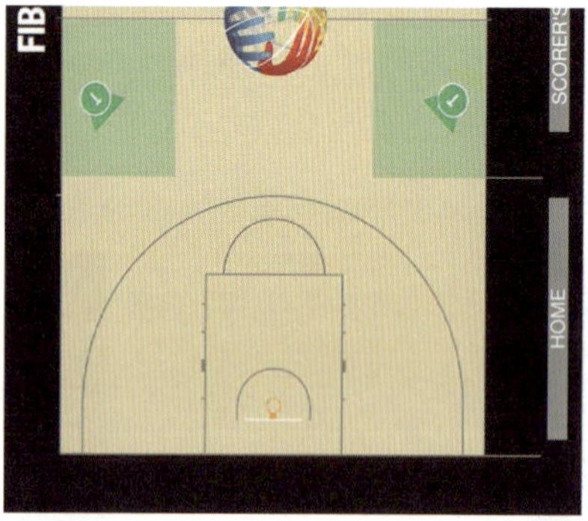

Diagram 16:
Trail working area is between team bench area line and centre line. If ball moves to close to strong side sideline, T should take one-two steps on the court to maintain wide angle.

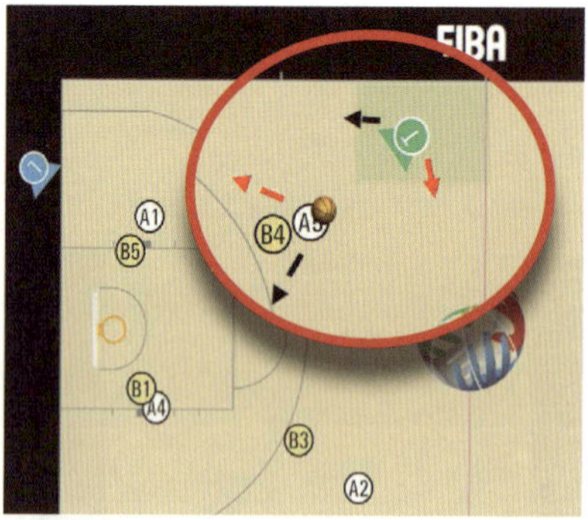

Diagram 17:
Whenever T is straight-lined, assess which side the player will move next. When player moves T should react and take cross step to the opposite direction of the players.

2.7.2 追踪裁判的位置

目标：明确追踪裁判的执裁位置和覆盖区域。

追踪裁判的工作区域位于球队席区域界线到中线之间。追踪裁判在场上要与队员保持适当的距离，这样他可以监控场上大多数的状况以对队员的动作进行预判。追踪裁判通常位于比赛场地内执裁。

当球向追踪裁判负责的边线运行时，他应该向场内移动，并保持开角观察。当面前有运球队员时，追踪裁判应当积极预判运球队员可能前进的方向。当运球队员向一侧移动时，追踪裁判应当运用交叉步向另一侧移动，这被称为“追踪裁判的交叉步”。当这个比赛片段结束，追踪裁判应当回到他位于边线附近的站位地点。

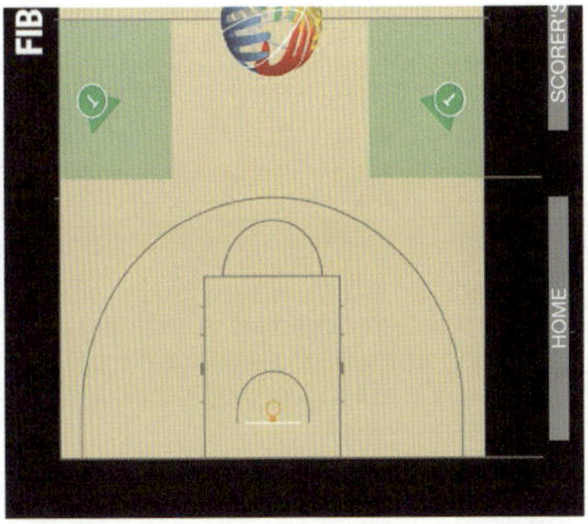

图 16：
追踪裁判工作区域位于球队席区域界线到中线之间，如果球靠近强侧边线，T应当使用一到两步的交叉步移动获得开角观察

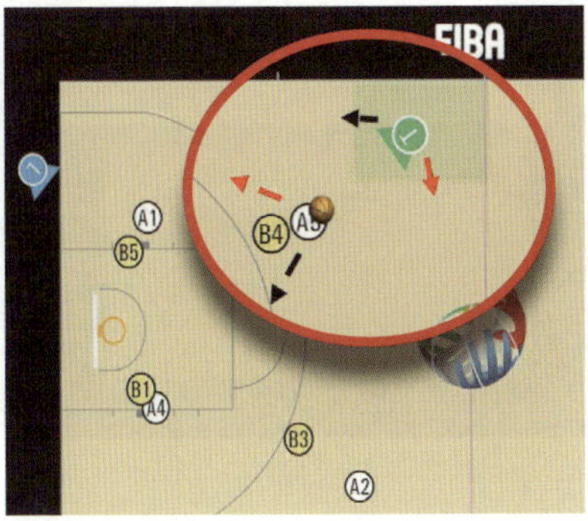

图 17：
无论何时，当 T 处于观察直线时，应当预判队员随后将朝哪边移动。当队员朝一侧移动时，追踪裁判应采用交叉步朝队员移动的反方向移动

2.7.3 CENTRE POSITION

Target: To identify proper working area and coverage in the Centre positon.

Centre working area is between top of the free throw circle and the imaginary "bottom of the free throw line circle". Practically speaking, this means the free throw line extended, a couple steps up, a couple steps down. The Centre working area is normally always on the court.

Any play on the weak side towards the basket is the Centre's primary. The Centre has to remember to be ready to make the call when there is illegal contact or action. If the Centre misses the illegal contact and is passive, this will force the Lead to be more active and in the worst case scenario, will result in "Lead cross calls" (trusting Lead & active Centre).

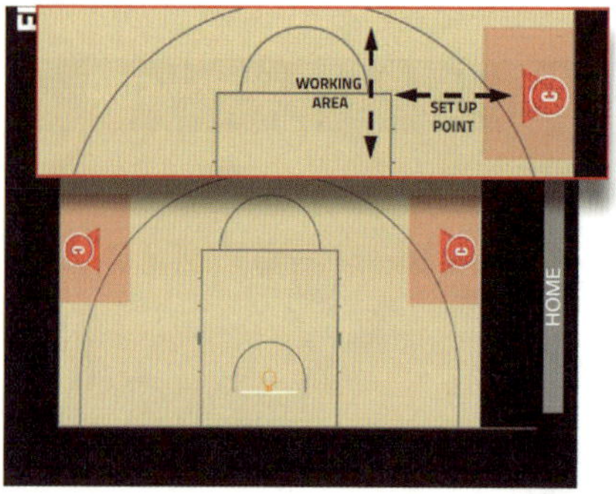

Diagram 18:
Centre's set-up position is at free throw line extended and working area from top of the free throw circle to the imaginary bottom of the free throw circle.

When there is a weak side drive to the basket, the Centre should take a step(s) on the court diagonally towards the centre line, or the same principle as with the Trail. Whenever a player moves in one direction, the Centre should move in the other direction. This is called "Centre cross step". There will always be a moment when the C is straight lined at the start of the drive, but this is only momentary and is minimized with the cross step.

2.7.3 中央裁判的位置

目标：明确中央裁判的执裁位置和覆盖区域。

中央裁判的工作区域位于罚球半圆的顶部和假想的罚球半圆的底部之间。从实践上说，这就是罚球线延长线上下两步的区域。中央裁判的工作区域保持在场地内。

任何弱侧朝向球篮的动作都属于中央裁判的职责。中央裁判要准确判罚职责内的非法接触或行为。如果中央裁判漏掉了非法接触或者比较消极，这将迫使前导裁判更加积极活跃并处于一个糟糕的观察视角，甚至会出现“前导裁判的跨区交叉宣判”（信任的前导裁判和积极的中央裁判）。

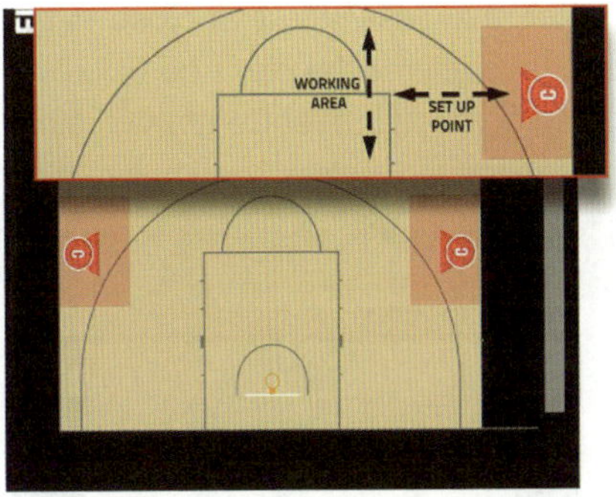

图 18：
中央裁判的工作区域位于罚球半圆的顶部和假想的罚球半圆的底部之间

当弱侧有队员突破时，中央裁判要向上线移动，这同样适用于追踪裁判。中央裁判的移动方向应当与运动员的突破方向相反。这被称作“中央裁判的交叉步”。中央裁判与队员形成一条线的情况时有发生，这只是短暂的瞬间，可以通过微调脚步来调整。

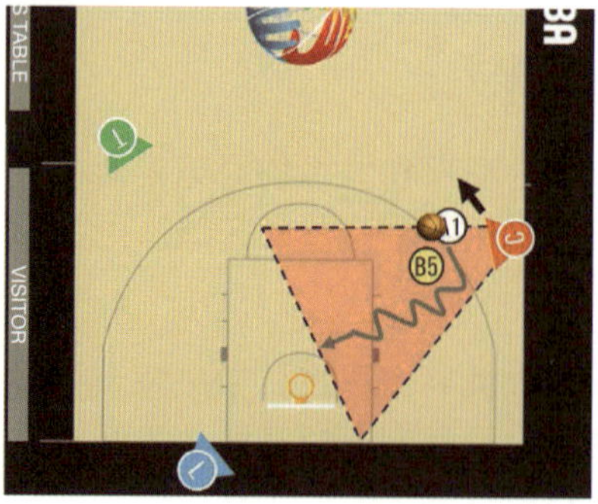

Diagram 19:
Ball on the weak side and C prepares to referee the drive to the basket (mentally ready to take cross step).

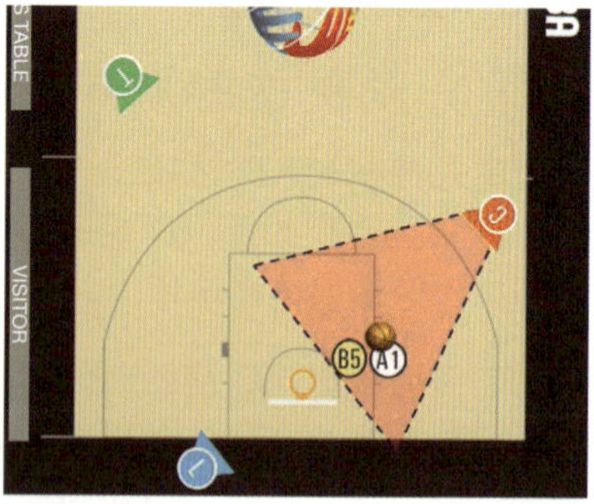

Diagram 20:
Dribbler moved to the left and C correctly cross step(s) to the right and maintains the open angle.

In case of trap situation in the frontcourt on the weak side and close to the centre line, C moves closer to the centre line to referee the play ("go wherever you need to referee the play"). After the trap situation is over Centre will return to the normal position at the free throw line extended, unless Lead has rotated during the trap (although should have rotated before the trap).

Diagram 21:
When there is a trap close to the centre line on the weak side of the court C needs to move closer to the centre line in order to cover the play properly, but this is not rotation (unless L is rotating).

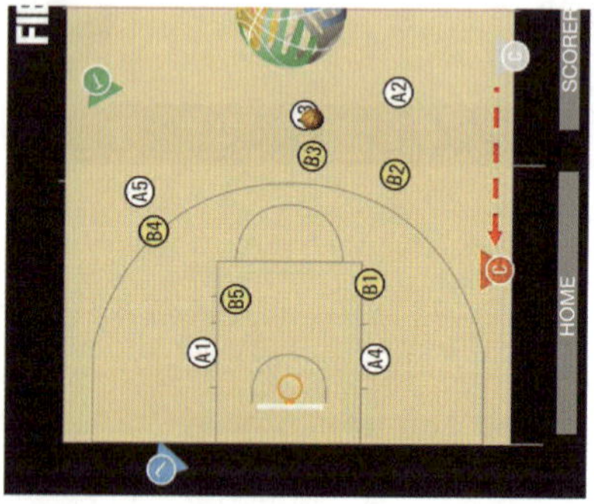

Diagram 22:
After the trap is over C will return to initial position and working area at the free throw line extended (unless L has rotated during the trap – first option).

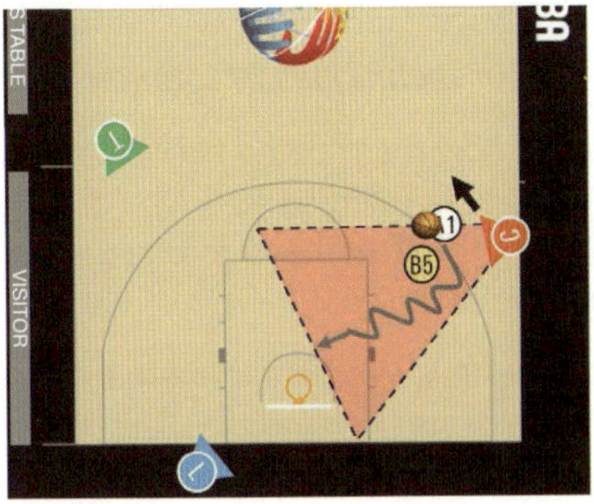

图 19：
当球位于弱侧，C 做好执裁向球篮突破的准备（思想上做好交叉步的准备）

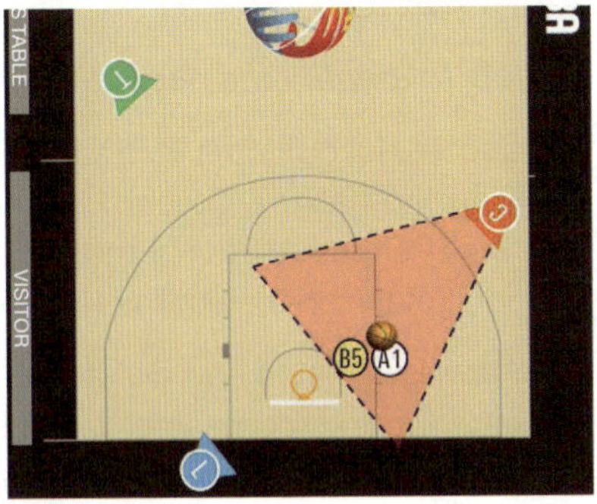

图 20：
运球队员向左侧移动，C 正确地向右做侧交叉步并保持开角

当出现弱侧靠近中线位置的包夹情况时，中央裁判应当靠近中线以观察比赛（“去你该去的地方以监控比赛”）。包夹结束后，中央裁判立刻返回罚球线延长线的常规位置。除非在包夹发生时，前导裁判已经发动了轮转（本应该可以在包夹发生前发动轮转）。

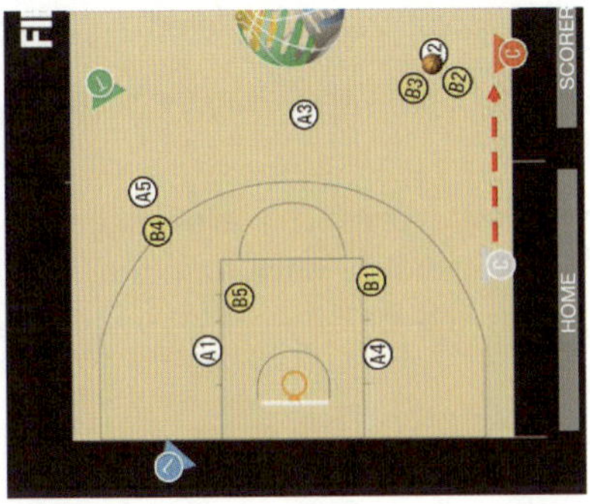

图 21：
当靠近弱侧中线出现包夹情况时，C 需要移动靠近中线位置以监控比赛，但这不是轮转（除非前导裁判发动）

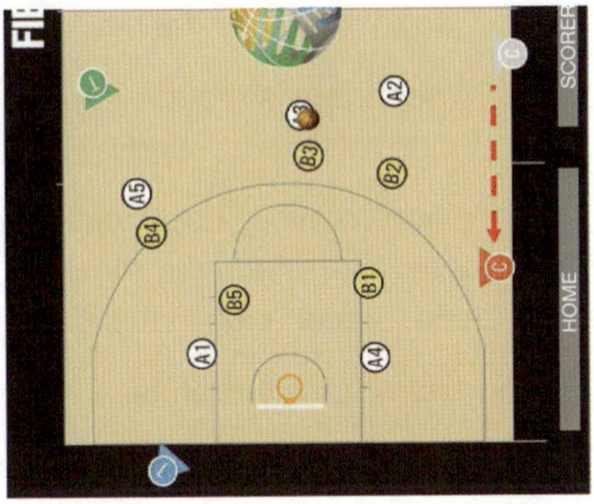

图 22：
当包夹结束时，C 应当立即返回罚球线延长线的常规位置（除非包夹发生时，前导裁判已经发动轮转——第一选择）

2.8 ROTATION

Target: To identify the need, time and proper techniques of rotation.

The successful outcome of 3PO depends on how many of the play situations involving the ball are covered by the strong side referees (L & T). For that reason, 3PO has rotational movements that allows the Lead to change the position (rotate) on the endline to the other side of the court.

Lead always initiates and dictates the rotation. It is very important that Lead is always looking for reasons to rotate (not reasons not to rotate). This active mind-set keeps 3PO coverage active in the frontcourt ensuring two referees are on ball side as much as possible.

Following techniques will assist with a successful rotation: (1) proper distance to rotate (close down), (2) proper timing to rotate (when ball moves to the weak side), and (3) proper technique (assess, move sharply, no hesitation).

Rotation in summary:

1. Ball moves to the middle of the court (Zone/Rectangle 2) -> Lead closes down.
2. Ball moves to the weak side (outside Zone/Rectangle 2) -> A) Lead rotates to the weak side and B) Trail rotates to the new Centre position.
3. Lead has completed the rotation and is ready to referee the play -> Centre rotates to the new Trail position. Rotation is completed.
4. When there is a quick shot or a drive from the weak side, there should be no rotation initiated by Lead.
5. When rotating, Lead walks sharply (never runs). This allows Lead to abort the rotation in the case of a quick shot or drive from the weak side, or a change in the direction of the play.

Rotation has 3 different phases:

1. **Phase 1: Close Down** When the ball is in the middle of the court (rectangle 2), Lead should move to the close down position in order to be ready to rotate when the ball moves to the weak side (outside of rectangle 2).

   If ball returns back to the strong side, Lead will kick out to the normal set-up position.

2.8 轮转

目标：明确轮转的需要、时机和恰当的技巧。

3 人执裁运用的成功与否，取决于前导裁判和追踪裁判能够负责多少球侧的比赛情况（L 和 T）。就是由于这个原因，3 人执裁才会有轮转，使得前导裁判从端线的一侧移动到另一侧（轮转）。

轮转总是由前导裁判发起。因此，前导裁判总是在不断寻找发动或中断轮转的理由（没有理由就不轮转）。这种保持活跃的精神状态，得以使强侧和球侧能够尽可能地重合。

成功的轮转需要一定的技巧：（1）恰当的距离（轮转发动区）；（2）恰当的时机（当球运行到弱侧）；（3）恰当的技巧（预判、快速移动、不要犹豫）。

轮转的步骤：

1. 球位于靠近中场的位置（中间区域 /2 区）→前导裁判位于轮转发动点；
2. 球移动到弱侧（超越了中间区域 /2 区）→ A) 前导裁判轮转到弱侧，B) 追踪裁判变成新的中央裁判。
3. 前导裁判已经完成轮转并做好了执裁比赛的准备→中央裁判变成新的追踪裁判，轮转完成。
4. 当在弱侧出现快速投篮或突破时，前导裁判不需要发动轮转；
5. 当轮转时，前导裁判快走（不要跑）。这使他可以在弱侧出现快速投篮、突破或攻防转换时，可以终止轮转。

轮转有 3 个不同的阶段：

1. **第一阶段：轮转发动点** 当球运行到场地中央（2 区）时，前导裁判应当移动到轮转发动点的位置，以做好球移动到弱侧（超越了 2 区）的准备。

   如果球又回到强侧，那么前导裁判回到正常的执裁位置。

Note: Close down position is not the position to referee the play. If there is a drive to the basket or a shot, Lead in close down position should move out in order to have proper distance and angle for the play.

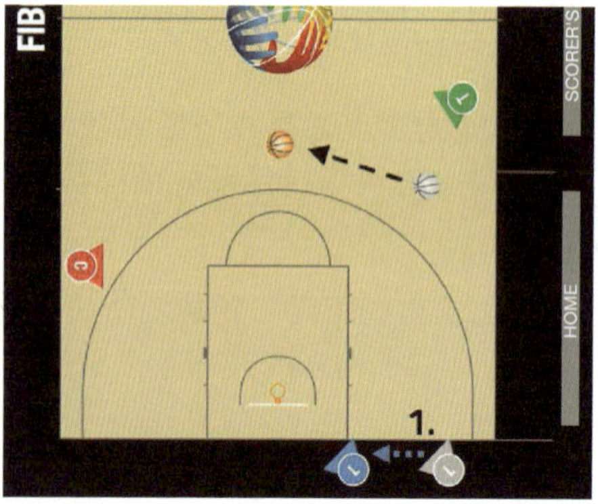

Diagram 23:
Ball moves and remains at rectangle 2 – Lead moves to close down position.

2. **Phase 2: Rotation by Lead & Trail** When the ball moves to the weak side, Lead starts the rotation as soon as possible. At the same time, Trail moves into the new Centre position.

    a. **Rotation by Lead – Scan the Paint** During rotation Lead should walk swiftly, scanning the paint (actively refereeing all the time). If there are players in the paint, they are normally Lead's primary.

    b. **Rotation by Trail to Centre position** As soon as the Trail has ensured that the Centre has picked up the ball on the weak side, the Trail should re-focus their vision and pick up the new weak side post play before starting the rotation. Studies have indicated that this is one of the weakest links during the rotation procedure, because often Trail remains locked in with the ball whilst rotating and without first re-focusing vision onto the weak side action.

注意：轮转发动点不是裁判员执裁的工作区域。如果有朝向球篮的运球或投篮时，位于轮转发动点位置的前导裁判应当迅速离开，以获得更好的距离和视角观察比赛。

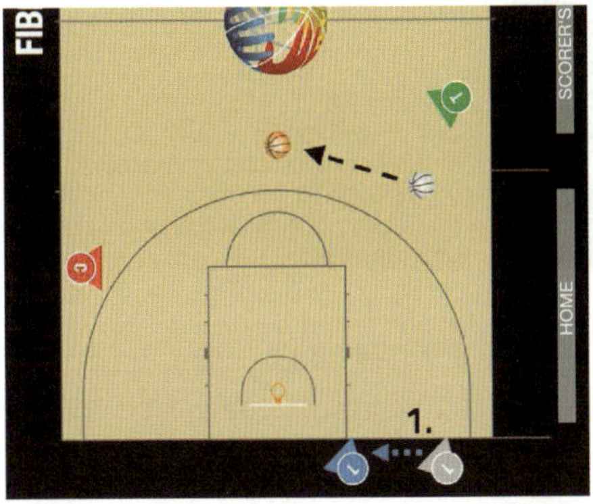

图 23：
球移动到 2 区，前导裁判移动到轮转发动点位置

2. **第二阶段：由前导裁判和追踪裁判发动轮转** 当球运行到弱侧，前导裁判尽快发动轮转。追踪裁判迅速移动到新的中央裁判的位置。

   a. **前导裁判发动——观察限制区** 在轮转中，前导裁判应该快步走，观察限制区（保持随时积极主动执裁）。如果有队员在限制区，通常是前导裁判的主要责任。

   b. **追踪裁判轮转到中央裁判的位置** 一旦追踪裁判确认中央裁判在弱侧接管了对球的监控之后，追踪裁判就应该把视线从球上移走，在轮转之前接管新的弱侧区域。研究表明，这是轮转的过程中最薄弱的环节之一，因为通常情况下追踪裁判的视线是锁定在球上的，而不是立即重新开始观察弱侧的矛盾。

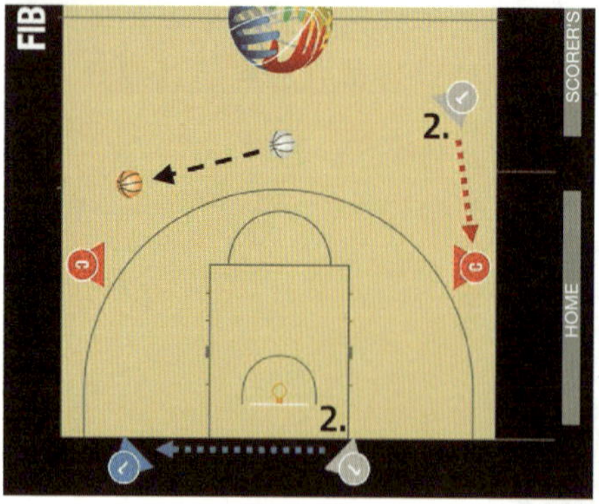

Diagram 24:
Ball moves to the weak side, L rotates and scans the paint or closest match-up. As soon as Centre has picked-up the ball, Trail shall pick-up the new weak side post play asap.

c. **Rotation "not completed" by Lead** When Leads uses the proper technique to rotate (early start, walking sharply), Lead will be able to stop the rotation any time and return back to the initial position (quick drive/shot from weak side).

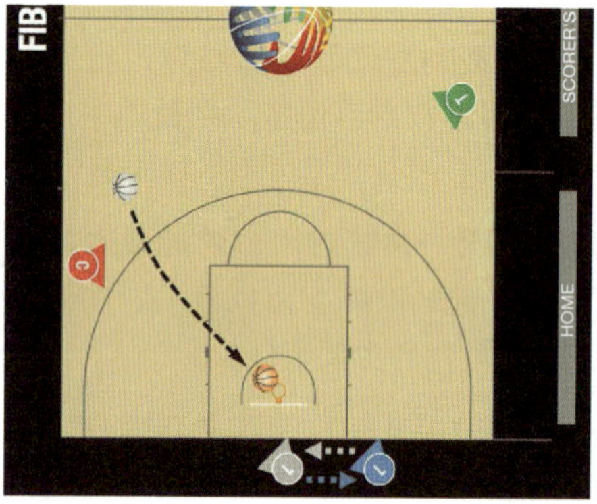

Diagram 25:
Quick drive/shot from the weak side and Lead is able to abort and return back to referee.

3. **Phase 3: Lead arrives to the ball side and Centre rotates to new Trail position**

After Lead has completed the rotation, Centre is the last person to rotate to the new Trail position.

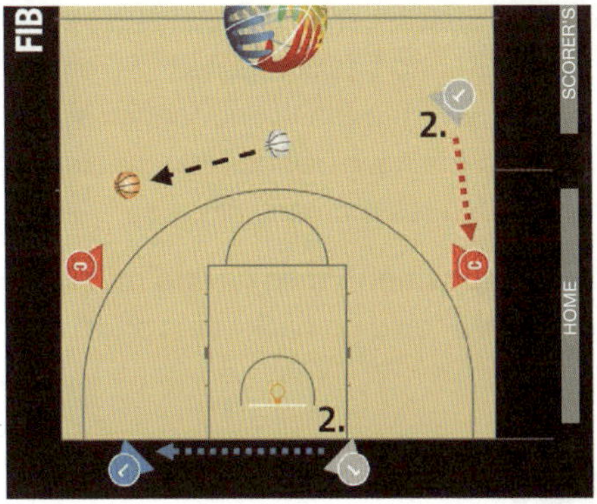

图 24：
球移动到弱侧，L 轮转时观察“油漆区”和攻防矛盾。当中央裁判接管球后，追踪裁判接管新的弱侧攻防情况

c. **中断轮转——前导裁判未完成** 当前导裁判运用恰当的技巧进行轮转时（早发动，快移动），前导裁判可以在任何时间中断轮转，并回到他的初始位置（当出现快速上篮或弱侧投篮的情况时）。

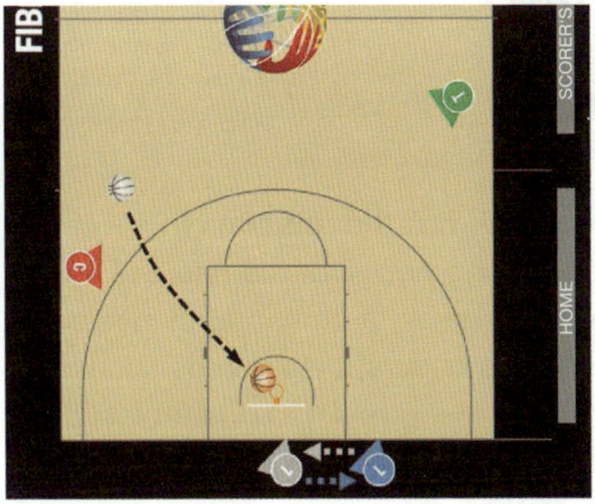

图 25：
出现弱侧快速上篮或投篮时，前导裁判可以中断轮转

3. 第三阶段：前导裁判移动到球侧，中央裁判轮转到新的追踪裁判位置。

当前导裁判完成了他的轮转之后，中央裁判移动到新的追踪裁判位置，成为最后一个完成轮转的人。

a. **Coverage by Centre & Lead** will stay in centre position and referee the ball and any play around it until Lead has completed the rotation and is ready to referee the play, and the play is no longer active. Only after this Centre will move to the new Trail position (rotate). As a result, there will always be two Centres momentarily.

b. **Rotation by Centre to the Trail position** When Centre moves up to the Trail position, this movement should be backwards and facing the basket at all times (45°).

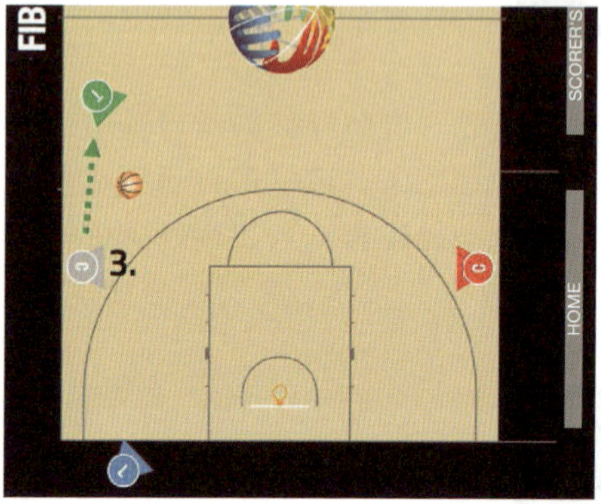

Diagram 26:
C will stay with the play until L has completed the rotation and is ready to referee. Old C is always the last one to move to the new T position (moving backwards) and now the rotation is completed.

4. **Misbalance – "partners do not pick-up" the rotation** While it should be avoided, there will be times when not all of the referees will be aware that there is a rotation in progress, and then a change in the direction of play occurs. Where this occurs, the referees should not panic as there are two options to adjust properly during a breakdown in the rotation while in transition.

   a. **Option 1: New Lead & Centre** to look across at each other and use voice to correct the imbalance (Diagram 27).

   b. **Option 2: New Trail** looks up and fills the gap. This may mean running diagonally across the court (Diagram 28).

a. **前导裁判和中央裁判覆盖的区域** 中央裁判保持原来位置继续观察场上的有球区域，一直持续到前导裁判完成轮转并进入新的监控区域，且比赛不再活跃时。只有在这之后，中央裁判再移动到新的追踪裁判位置（轮转）。这样做的结果，会使场上暂时性地出现两名中央裁判。

b. 轮转完成后，**中央裁判移动到追踪裁判的位置** 当中央裁判移动到追踪裁判的位置时，应向后移动，并且始终面向球篮（45°）。

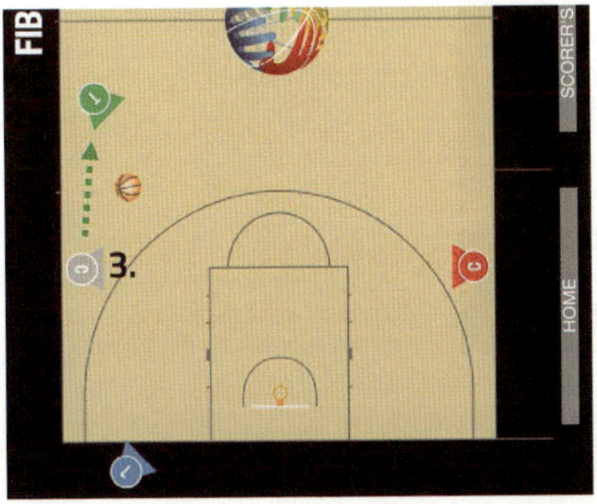

图 26：
C 保持观察，直到 L 完成轮转并接管比赛。原来的 C 最后移动到新的 T 位置后，轮转完成

4. **第四阶段：失衡情况——“同伴没有接上”轮转** 当然，这种情况应当是极力避免的。但是比赛中会有同伴没有意识到轮转情况的发生，而此情况到攻守转换时才被发现。如何处理这种情况？不必惊慌，裁判员们在攻防转换中有两次机会弥补轮转失误。

a. **选择 1：新的前导裁判和中央裁判** 相互观察彼此位置，使用声音信号来修正位置错误。（图 27）

b. **选择 2：新的追踪裁判** 发现问题，并进入修正的位置。这可能导致横穿场地的情况。（图 28）

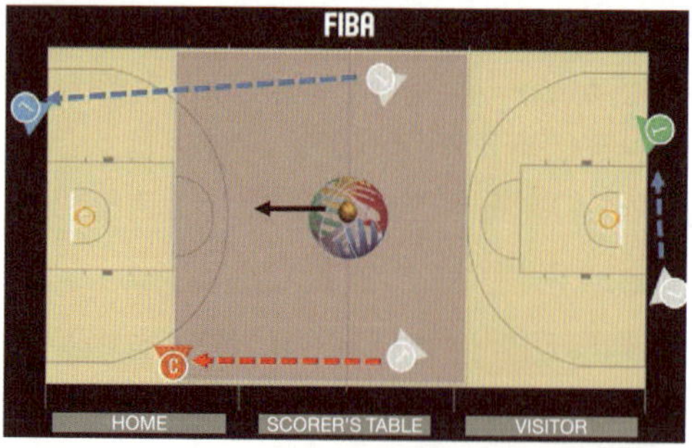

Diagram 27:
New C & L should always control the court in transition, before they arrive at the free throw line extended on the frontcourt.

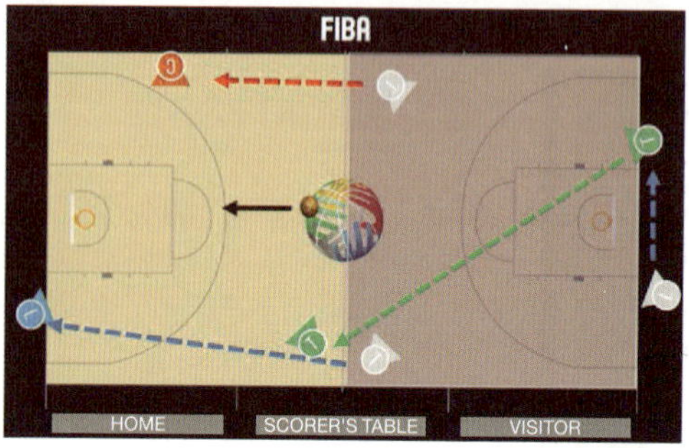

Diagram 28:
Second option is that new T balances the court coverage by crossing the court diagonally, on the backcourt.

2.9 TRANSITION / LEAD

Target: To identify proper working area and coverage in the Lead positon

During transition, the new Lead should be ahead of the play and arrive to the baseline in four seconds or less, and should be in a position ready to referee. The new Lead should also be in good position to referee the play throughout transition down the floor. This is only possible when the following correct techniques are applied:

a. Stay with the previous play before the new transition – namely, wait until the ball has entered the basket in the case of a successful shot for goal or when a defensive player has gained control of a rebound;

b. After turning with a power step, be sure to face the court all the time (when done properly, the referee should also able to pick-up the game clock);

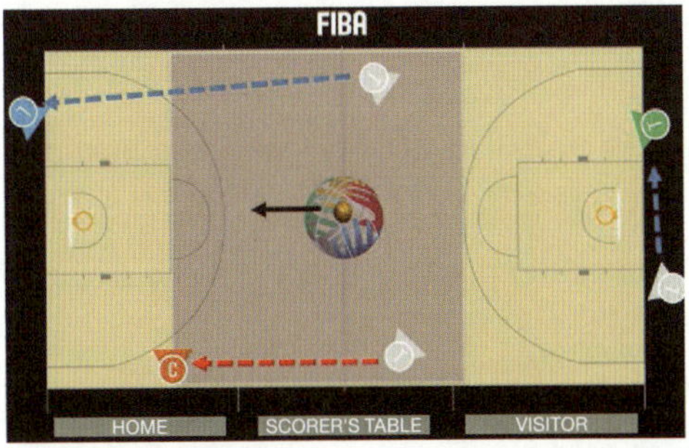

图 27：
在转换中，新的 C 和 L 应该在到达前场的罚球线延长线之前持续监控比赛

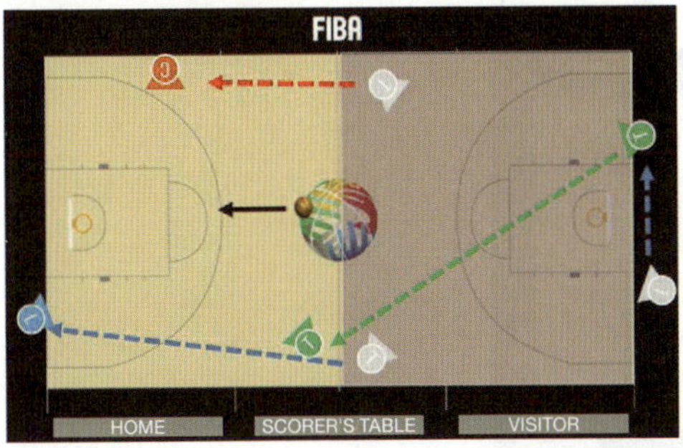

图 28：
第二个选择是新的 T 可以通过在后场穿插到另一侧来保持场上的位置平衡

2.9 攻防转换与前导裁判

目标：明确前导裁判的工作区域和视野覆盖。

攻防转换中，新的前导裁判一般要在 4 秒之内移动到对面端线，并做好执裁准备。前导裁判在移动过程中也要保证良好的位置来执裁。下列技巧是能够良好宣判的重要所在：

a. 完全结束上一比赛片段后再转换位置——也就是说，要等投篮的球完全进入球篮或防守队获得篮板球；

b. 在转身用力蹬地跑向端线后，保持面向球场（当正确完成后，还应该保持对比赛计时钟的监控）；

c. Start transition with full speed and maintain it until arriving at the baseline;

d. Face the court during the entire transition (actively looking for next play to come and refereeing the defence);

e. Run straight to the baseline to set-up position (keeping same distance from the play all the way) – “out-side/out-side” angle;

f. Stop on the baseline with “one-two” count in a stationary position, and be ready to referee the play when it starts.

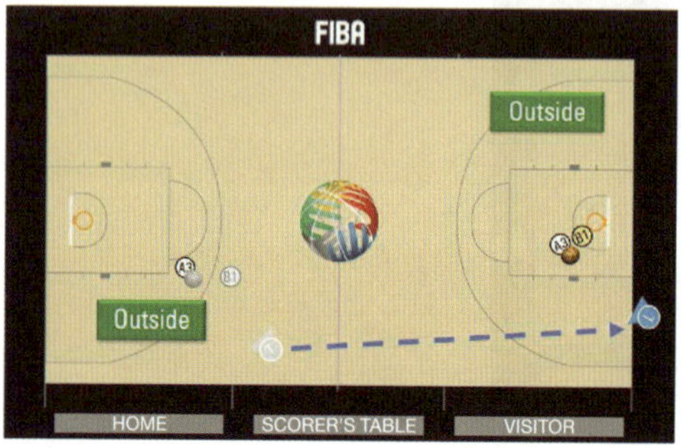

Diagram 29:
L moves correctly with straight line to the endline maintaining the same distance from the play – speed and size of the players remains same from the start to the end.

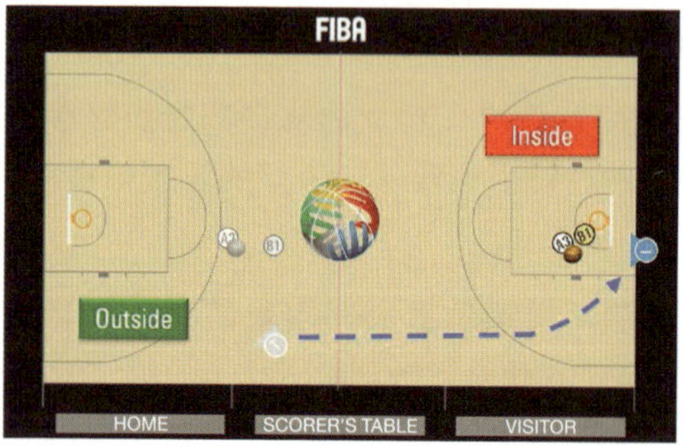

Diagram 30:
L curves incorrectly close to the basket and the play is coming at L. The angle changes completely because players look bigger and faster.

c. 全速启动并保持速度直到到达端线；

d. 在整个转换过程中要面对球场（动态地观察接下来的比赛和执裁防守）；

e. 直线跑到端线位置并建立初始位置（保持与比赛的固定距离）——保持开角；

f. 停在端线的一个静立位置并默数“一、二”，并准备再次执裁接下来的比赛。

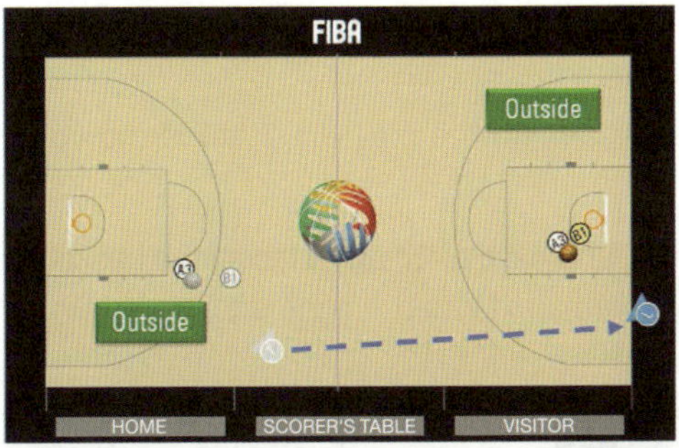

图 29:
L 正确地沿直线跑动，抵达端线并与比赛保持适当的距离——队员的速度和体形自始至终保持一致

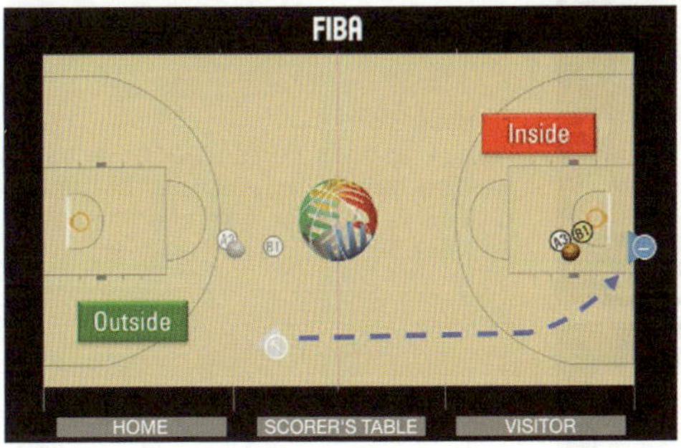

图 30:
L 错误地以曲线跑向球篮，使得比赛朝 L 而来。由于队员看起来更大更快，导致视角完全变化

2.10 TRANSITION / TRAIL

Target: To identify proper working area and coverage in the Trail position

During transition, the new Trail should always trail the play (behind the play – not in line or in front of the play). This way the Trail is able to easily control the clocks and analyse the next possible plays to come. This is only possible when the following correct techniques are implemented:

Wait behind the baseline until the ball is either passed to a teammate on the court after a made basket and the thrower-in has advanced on to the court (the new Trail should wait to have a minimum of 3 meters distance from the ball before they step on to the court);

Always maintain a proper distance behind the play – 1-2 steps (no yo-yo running);

Be the last to arrive in the front court, and have a 45° angle facing the basket (all players should be between straight arms extended = right/left side sideline & left/right side centre line).

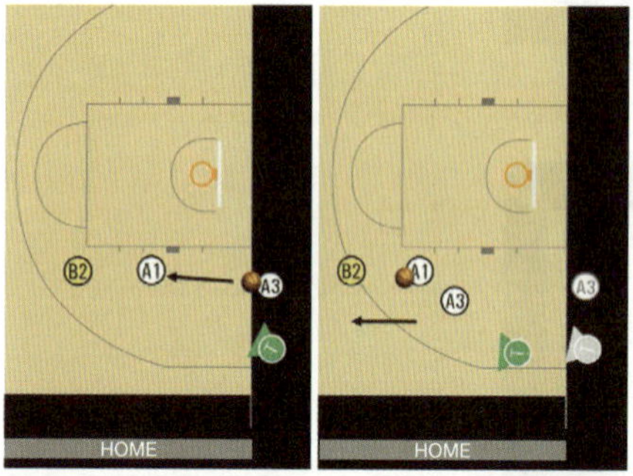

Diagram 31:
New T applies correct techniques by waiting behind the endline that ball is passed to the team mate after the basket and the thrower-in has advanced to the court.

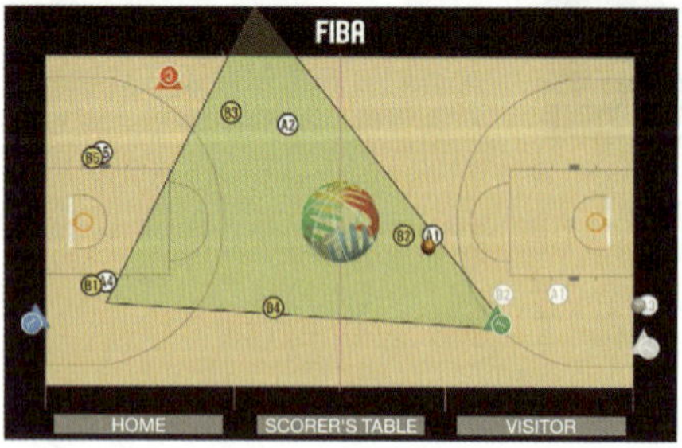

Diagram 32:
T maintains the proper distance always behind the play (no yo-yo running) facilitating the steady wide angle and T is able to control the clocks and see the set-ups on the frontcourt.

2.10 攻防转换与追踪裁判

目标：明确追踪裁判的执裁位置和覆盖区域。

攻防转换中，新的追踪裁判应当始终位于比赛的后面（不要超越或平行于比赛）。这样追踪裁判可以轻松监控计时钟并分析下一次可能的对抗的到来。这些只有在应用正确的技术时才有可能实现：

中篮或后场的掷球入界中，追踪裁判要站在端线以外等待球掷入场地。球掷入场地前，裁判员应当保持在距离球 3 米的位置观察比赛。

总是保持在比赛后方 1~2 步的适当距离（不要折返跑）。

最后一个进入前场，并保持面向球篮 45° 的站立位置（所有队员应在伸直的两臂延长线之间 = 右侧 / 左侧的边线和左侧 / 右侧的中线之间）。

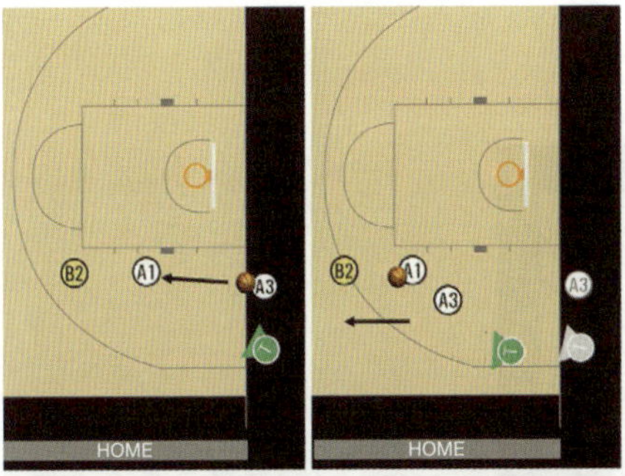

图 31：
新的 T 采用了正确的技术，在球中篮后等在端线后边，直到掷球入界的队员将球传给队友，然后开始向前场移动

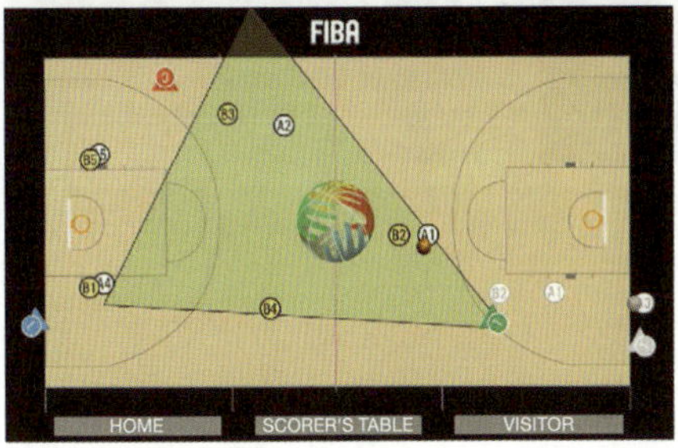

图 32：
T 一直位于比赛的后方（不要折返跑移动），并保持适当的距离以维持固定的开角，并且他能监控计时钟和观察到前场的设置

2.11 TRANSITION / CENTRE

Target: To identify proper working area and coverage in the Centre positon

During the transition from Centre to Centre, the referee in question has to follow these techniques:

a. Stay with the previous play before the new transition. Namely, wait until the ball has entered the basket in the case of a successful attempt for goal, or until a defensive player has gained control of a rebound;

b. Face the court during the entire transition (actively looking for next play to come and refereeing defence);

c. Run straight to the frontcourt free throw line extended (set-up position);

d. When a transition play is advancing on the weak side, Centre might need to stop momentarily and referee the play (keep distance from the play – anticipate).

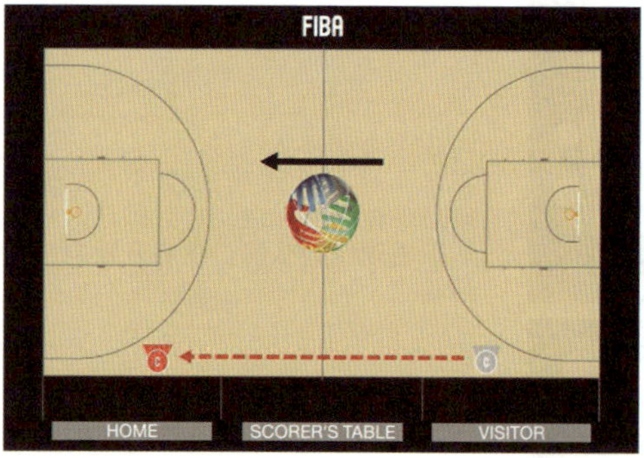

Diagram 33:
Centre normally moves in the transition from backcourt to frontcourt free throw line extended facing court covering possible any weak side transition.

2.11 攻防转换与中央裁判

目标：明确中央裁判的工作区域和视野覆盖。

从中央裁判转换到中央裁判的过程中，应当运用如下技巧：

a. 在新的攻防转换之前一直保持对前一个比赛片断的监控。也就是说，要等到一次投篮得分尝试，球完全进入球篮或者一名防守队员已经获得篮板球之后；

b. 转换的过程中全程面向场地（积极观察比赛的发展和执裁防守）；

c. 直线跑到前场罚球线延长线的位置（初始位置）；

d. 如果比赛在转换过程中发展到弱侧，那么中央裁判要立即停止移动，准备判罚（通过预判保持与比赛的合适距离）。

图 33:
中央裁判通常的移动位置是从后场到前场罚球线延长线的位置，应当面向场地监控所有弱侧的攻防转换

2.12 FAST BREAK

Target: To identify proper coverage and Lead-Centre cooperation during a fast break

During the fast break, it is important to understand that the Centre has to be active and has 50% of the coverage (weak side).

Any action or contact on the weak side should be covered by Centre, and any action on the strong side by Lead. This is the beauty of 3PO when it works properly.

It is good to practise when running from Trail to Lead in transition to automatically identify where the Centre is on the other side of the court. When this becomes a standard procedure, it will also automatically happen during the fast break when time is more limited.

The Lead and Centre need to run at full speed, analyse when the play will start, and then stop and referee the play by focusing on the defence (referee defence). The weak point in coverage during the fast break is when the new Lead curves under the basket and tries to referee the action on the weak side. This destroys the concept of 3PO as each referee is responsible for their own primary and there should be no need for secondary.

It is important that the Centre quickly arrives in the front court at the free throw line extended to have the best coverage for a possible basket interference or goaltending (see also *"2.20 Basket interference & goaltending"* for more details).

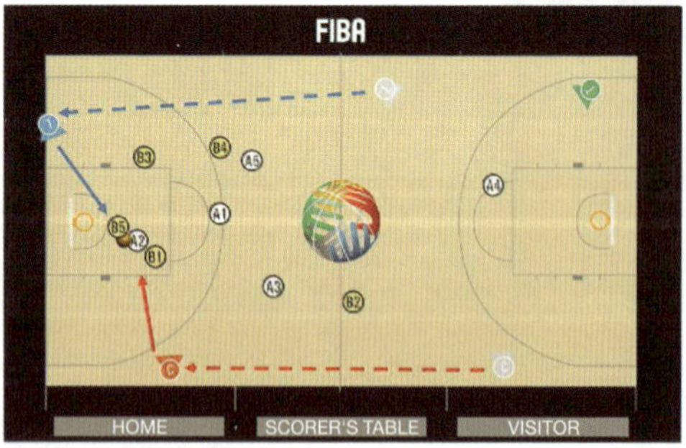

Diagram 34:
C has to run fast in every fast break. It is important that both L & C are able to have a stationary position to referee when the play starts. This is normally a dual coverage situation.

2.12 快攻

目标：明确快攻中适当的区域分工以及前导—中央裁判的配合。

在快攻中，明确中央裁判应该积极主动并且负责 50% 的区域（弱侧）。

任何弱侧的动作与接触都应由中央裁判观察，同时强侧的动作应由前导裁判负责。这就是正确运行 3 人执裁的精彩之处。

由追踪裁判变为前导裁判的转换过程中，能自然地感觉到中央裁判在场地另一侧的位置是需要勤于练习的，因为这需要成为一种标准的程序，即使当时间有限的快攻发生时，也能自然而然地形成。

追踪裁判和前导裁判需要全速奔跑，分析动作开始的时机，而后停下通过注意防守来观察动作（执裁防守）。在快攻中的区域分工，切忌新的前导裁判切入篮下试图去观察弱侧的动作，这打破了 3 人执裁的概念，即每名裁判员应负责各自的主要责任区，而并非监控次要责任区。

中央裁判应当快速跑到前场的罚球线延长线处，寻找最好的视野角度去观察可能出现的干扰得分或干涉得分（详细参见“2.20 干扰得分与干涉得分”）。

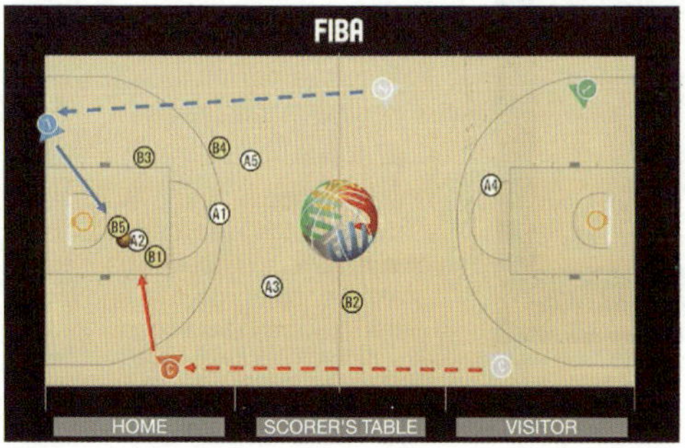

图 34:
C 在快攻中必须全力奔跑，L 和 C 在快攻中静立宣判十分重要，通常情况下快攻是两名裁判员共同覆盖的

2.13 PRESS DEFENCE

Target: To identify proper coverage and Trail-Centre cooperation during a press.

When there is more than two opponent pair of players in the backcourt the Centre has to be active and help Trail to cover the play. If all the players are in the backcourt also the Lead has to adjust their position closer to the play ready to cover any potential long passes.

All players in the backcourt

Diagram 35:
T and C referee the action in the backcourt.

More than 4 opponent players in the backcourt

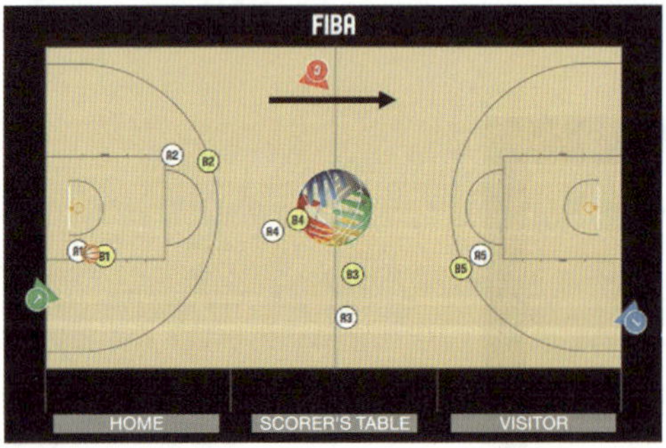

Diagram 36:
T referees behind the play. C takes a position close to centre line to referee players in front or backcourt. L takes position on the endline to referee players in frontcourt.

2.13 紧逼防守

目标：明确紧逼时适当的区域分工及追踪—中央裁判的配合。

当后场出现两对以上的攻防矛盾时，中央裁判必须积极观察并协助追踪裁判监控比赛。如果所有队员都在后场，那么前导裁判也需要调整他的位置，靠近比赛以便监控可能出现的长传。

所有队员都在后场

图 35：
T 和 C 执裁后场的比赛情况

超过四名对方队员在后场

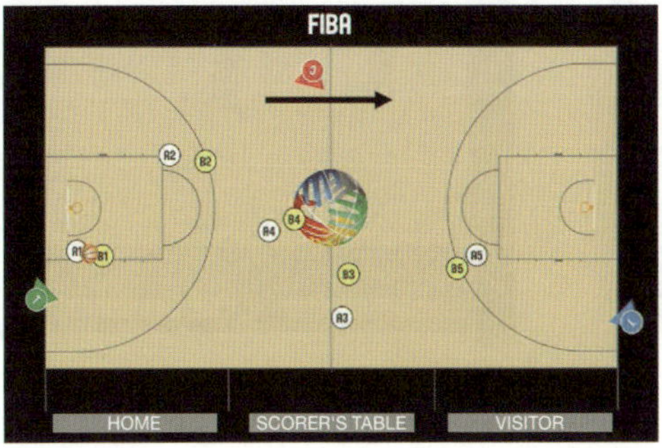

图 36：
T 在比赛后方执裁。C 占据靠近中线的位置并监控在前场或后场的队员。L 占据前场端线的位置并监控前场的队员

2.14 OUT-OF-BOUNDS & THROW-INS

Target: To understand coverage on out-of-bounds plays to ensure that only one referee always makes the "out-of-bounds" call.

3PO covers all of the boundary lines in the frontcourt. Only the Trail has two lines to cover. The basic rule is that Lead covers the baseline, Centre covers the weak side sideline, and Trail covers the strong side sideline and centre line.

When the game continues with a throw-in there should always be two referees (Lead & Trail) on the side of a throw-in.

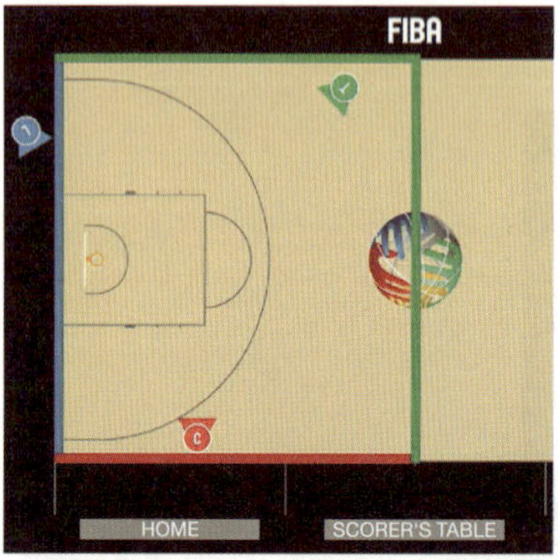

Diagram 37:
L & C has one boundary line to cover, while T has two lines (sideline and centreline).

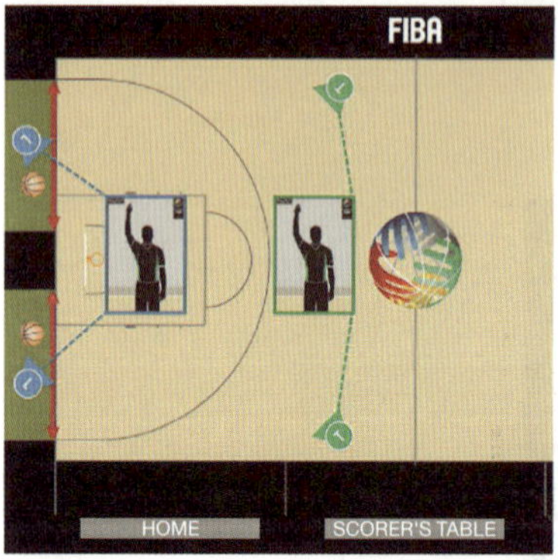

Diagram 38:
When the throw-in is on the frontcourt's endline between 3 point line and edge of the backboard, L's position is outside of the throwin spot (C has to be ready to cover weak side). T mirrors the "time-in" signal to the table.

Diagram 39:
When the throw-in is on the frontcourt's endline between 3 point line and sideline, L's position is between basket and throw-in spot. T mirrors the "time-in" signal to the table.

2.14 球出界与掷球入界

目标：理解球出界情况下的区域分工以及明确只应有一名裁判员做出“球出界”的宣判。

3 人执裁的观察范围覆盖了前场的所有界线。只有追踪裁判负责观察两条线。其基本原则为：前导裁判负责端线，中央裁判负责弱侧的边线，同时追踪裁判负责强侧的边线和中线。

当掷球入界恢复比赛时，掷球入界一侧总有两名裁判员（前导裁判和追踪裁判）。

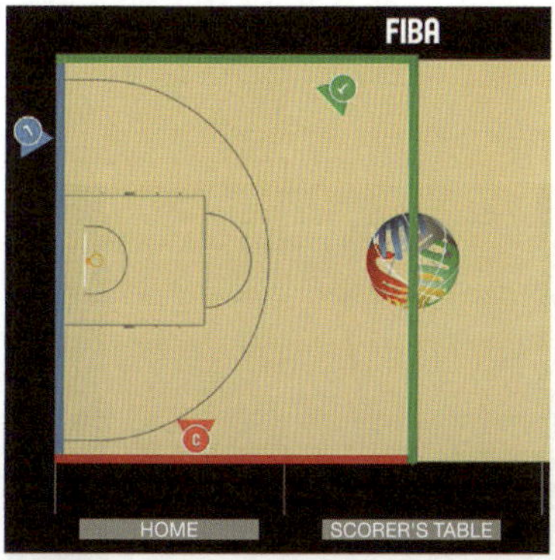

图 37：
L 和 C 各负责一条界线，T 负责两条界线（边线和中线）

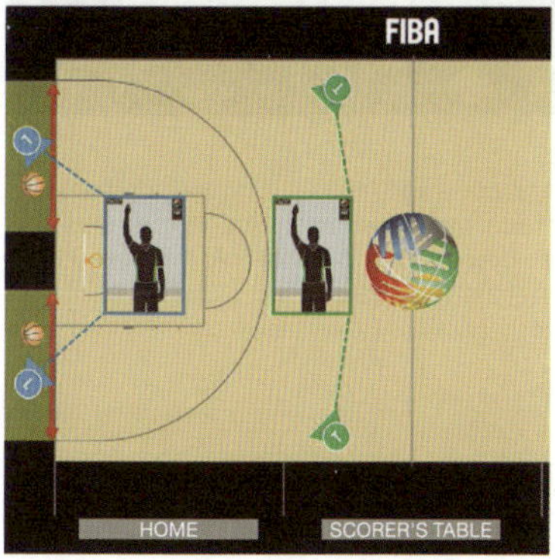

图 38：
当掷球入界地点位于前场 3 分线与篮板边界之间的端线处，L 的位置在掷球入界点的外侧（C 准备观察弱侧）。T 向记录台做出镜像的“开动计时钟”的手势

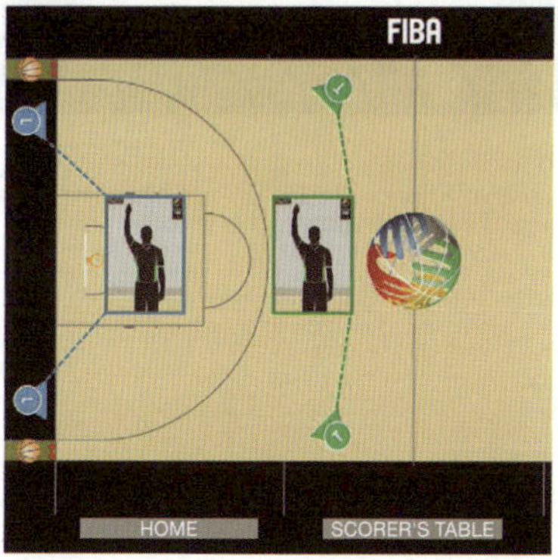

图 39：
当掷球入界地点位于前场 3 分线与边线之间的端线处，L 的位置在球篮与掷球入界点之间。T 向记录台做出镜像的“开动计时钟”的手势

2.15 SHOT COVERAGE (GENERAL & 3 POINTS ATTEMPTS)

Target: To identify and understand the coverage of each referee during shots for goal.

The basic principle is that the Lead has primary coverage on 2 point shots on the strong side in their primary area (as demonstrated below, blue area) and the Trail has primary coverage for all 3 point shots, and 2 point shots on the strong side. The Centre has primary coverage on all shots on the weak side (see Diagram 40).

Whenever there is dual coverage (restricted area, rectangle 2), the basic principle is that the respective referee covers their side of the play (see Diagram 41).

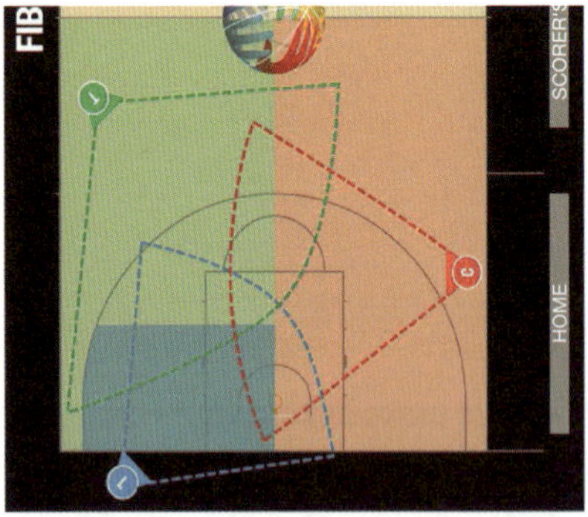

Diagram 40:
L has normally the primary coverage in blue area, T in green area and C in red area.

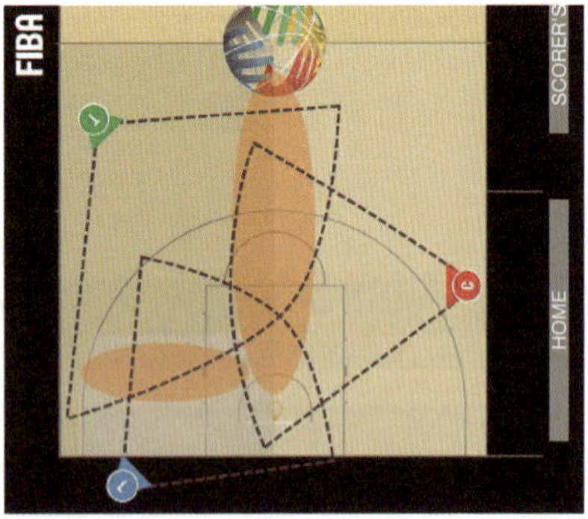

Diagram 41:
In dual coverage areas it is important that both referees have the discipline to process the entire play and try to focus only for their side of the defensive players.

2.15 投篮的区域分工（一般情况与 3 分试投）

目标：确认和理解在投篮情况下每名裁判员的区域分工。

基本原则是前导裁判负责强侧的任何 2 分投篮（如下图蓝色区域所示），追踪裁判负责所有的 3 分投篮以及强侧的 2 分投篮。中央裁判负责弱侧的所有投篮。（见图 40）

不管何时出现共管区（限制区，2 区），基本原则都是裁判员分别对各自的区域负主要责任。（见图 41）

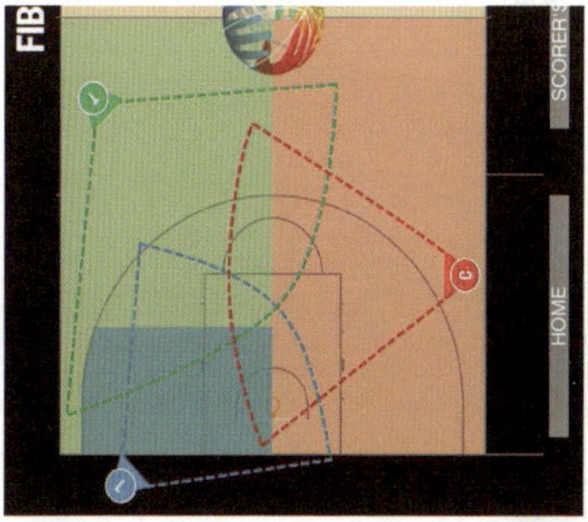

图 40：
通常 L 的主要责任区为蓝色区域，T 为绿色区域，C 为红色区域

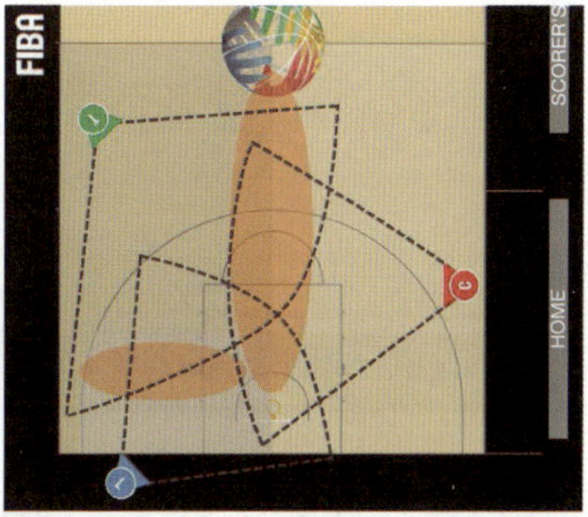

图 41：
在共管区域内，两名裁判员都有义务观察整个动作的发生并集中注意在他们一侧的防守队员

2.16 TIME-OUTS

After the table officials have notified the referees about the time-out request, normally the Trail or Centre closest to the table will signal the time-out.

Referees have three standard positions during the time-outs (always on the opposite side). They can select any of the three positions they feel are the most appropriate (Note: leave the ball on the court where the game will be resumed).

When a time-out has 20 seconds remaining, two referees will move close to the team bench areas in order to be ready to activate the teams to return back to the court when the 50 seconds warning signal sounds.

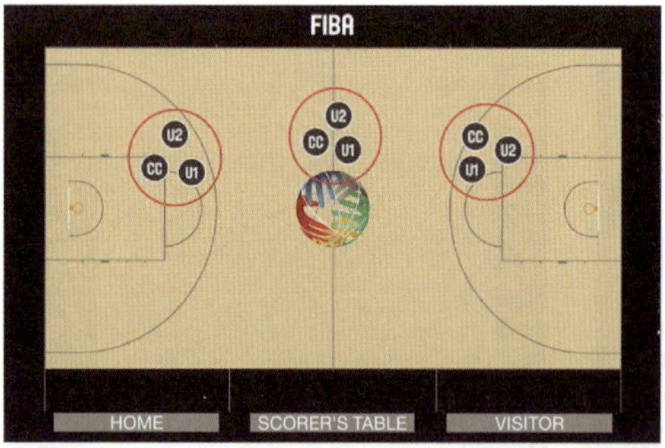

Diagram 42:
The three standard time-out positions, always in the opposite side.

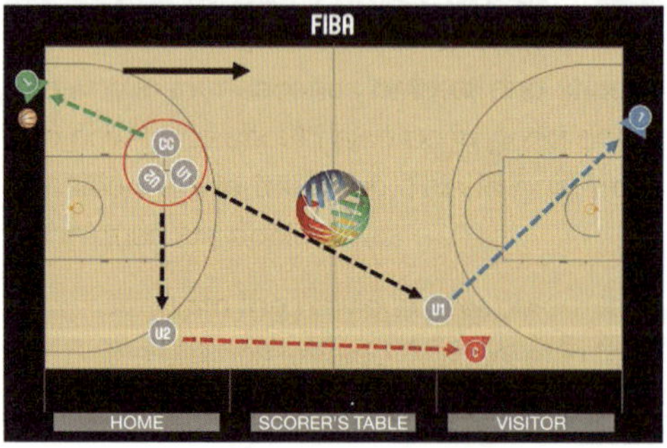

Diagram 43:
When 20 seconds remaining of the time-out, two referees move close to the team bench areas.

2.16 暂停

在记录台人员将暂停的请求告知裁判员后，通常由最靠近记录台的追踪裁判或中央裁判做出暂停信号。

在暂停期间，裁判员有三种标准的站位（总是在记录台对侧）。他们应选择他们感觉最适合的一种站位方法（注意：把球放置在比赛将要恢复的位置上）。

当暂停时间剩余 20 秒时，两名裁判员移动到球队席区附近，这是为了准备在 50 秒信号响起时提醒队员们做好准备回到场上。

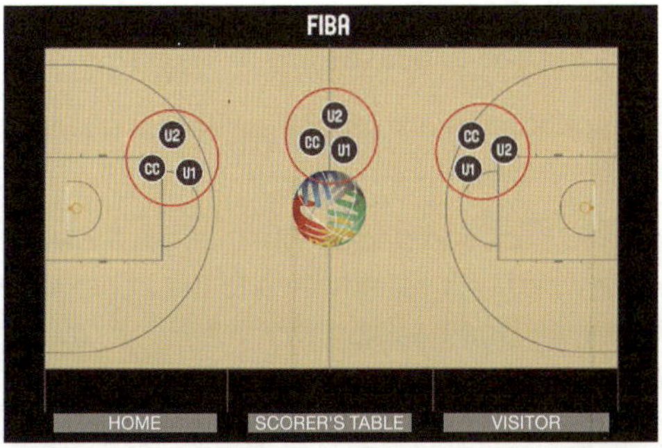

图 42：
暂停时三种标准的站立位置，位于对侧

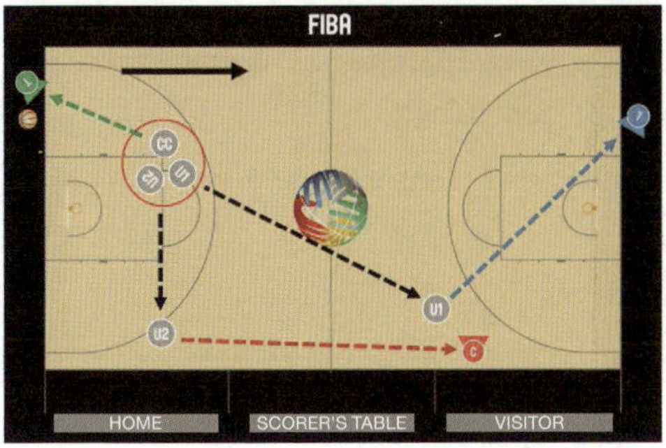

图 43：
当暂停还有 20 秒剩余时间，两名裁判员移动到靠近球队席区域的地方

Last 2 minutes (L2M) time-out protocol

(where a team has the opportunity to advance the ball to the frontcourt)

When the clock shows 2:00 minutes or less in the fourth quarter and in overtime when the team requesting the time-out is entitled to possession of the ball from its backcourt:

- Referees have three standard positions during the time-outs (always on the opposite side). They can select any of the three positions they feel are the most appropriate.
- During the time-out, the ball is to remain in the hands of the crew chief (this signals that a decision for the throw-in location is yet to be made).
- When a time-out has 20 seconds remaining, the crew chief and the one of the umpires will move close to the team bench areas. The crew chief will go to the team that is entitled to possession of the ball.
- When the 50 seconds signal sounds the officials will activate the teams to return back to the court.
- The crew chief will ask the head coach to decide whether the throw-in will remain in the backcourt or whether it will advance to the frontcourt. The crew chief will verbally confirm the decision with the Head Coach (e.g. "The throw-in will be in the back / front court."). The crew chief will show a signal to the location of the throw-in by pointing to and moving to that location for the throw-in. Verbal support of this will accompany the signal.
- The crew chief will normally administer the throw-in, with the other two referees adjusting their positions accordingly.
- The referees shall ensure that the shot clock is appropriately set (reset/ remain) before the throw-in.

2.17 SUBSTITUTIONS

Trail or Centre closest to the table will administer the substitutions. All substitutions should be completed as quickly as possible. As soon as all substitutions are completed the administering referee should make sure there is a correct number of players on the playing court and shall then communicate by establishing eye contact with the active referee with the ball.

最后 2 分钟（L2M）暂停规定

（球队有机会决定在前场掷球入界）

在第 4 节和每一决胜期的比赛计时钟显示 2:00 分钟或更少时，在后场拥有球权的队请求了暂停：

- 在暂停期间裁判员有三种标准的站立位置（位于对侧）。他们可以选择三个位置中任意一个合适的。
- 在暂停期间，球应该在主裁判的手里（这表明了掷球入界的地点还没有确定）。
- 当暂停时间还剩 20 秒时，主裁判和一名副裁判将移动到球队席区域。主裁判移动到有掷球入界球权的球队。
- 当 50 秒信号响起时，裁判员提醒队员们回到比赛场地。
- 主裁判应询问主教练决定接下来的掷球入界是在后场比赛停止时的地点执行或是在前场执行。主裁判需要口头重复主教练的决定（例如“掷球入界要在后 / 前场执行。”）。主裁判要用手势指明掷球入界的地点以及移动到该地点管理掷球入界。语言的提示要伴随着相应的手势。
- 通常由主裁判管理这次掷球入界，其他两名裁判员相应调整各自的位置。
- 主裁判应确保在掷球入界前，设置正确的进攻计时钟时间（复位 / 保持）。

2.17 替换

最靠近记录台的追踪裁判或中央裁判要管理替换。所有替换应尽可能快地完成。在替换一完成时，执行裁判应确认场上正确的队员数量，随后应与负责管理球的裁判员建立眼神交流。

Substitutions after a foul call

After the calling referee has finished the reporting to the table it is the responsibility of the new table side referee (Trail or Centre) to administer substitutions.

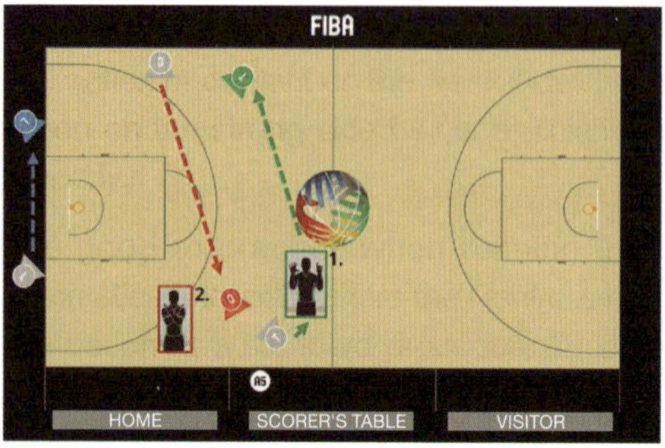

Diagram 44:
T has finished reporting and moves to a new position for free throws. New C will then administer substitutions.

2.18 EIGHT SECONDS & BACKCOURT VIOLATIONS

Normally Trail has the primary responsibility to count the 8 seconds. On all press situations Centre should be ready to assist the Trail (physically and mentally engaged with the play).

Trail also has the primary responsibility on all centre line violations. Sometimes the Centre can also help with possible backcourt violations when the ball is played on the weak side before returning to the backcourt.

2.19 SHOT CLOCK COVERAGE

Normally it is the outside referees (Trail and Centre) who have primary responsibility for shot clock violations. Also the Lead should be aware of the time on the shot clock and to be ready to assist Trail / Centre in their decisions. It is vital for referees to know when the shot clock period is nearing its end to be able to make correct decisions in shot clock situations.

At all times the active referee administering the throw-in should check the shot clock to be sure it is set correctly. This must be done before referee passes the ball to the thrower-in.

Note: When the backboard is equipped with yellow lighting along its perimeter at the top, the lighting takes precedence over the shot clock signal sound.

宣判一起犯规后的替换

在宣判犯规的裁判员完成向记录台的报告后，新的记录台侧的裁判员（追踪裁判或中央裁判）要负责管理替换。

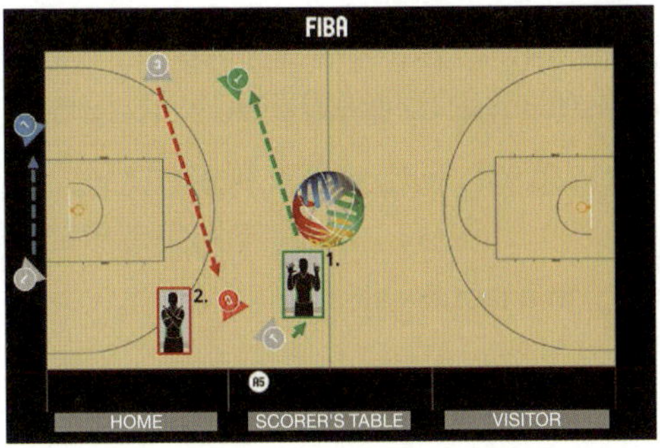

图 44:
T 在完成报告犯规后移动到了新的位置准备罚球程序。新的 C 随后管理替换

2.18 8 秒违例与球回后场违例

通常来说，追踪裁判对于 8 秒的计数负主要责任。在所有的紧逼情况中，中央裁判应随时准备去协助追踪裁判（身体和精神都要融入比赛）。

追踪裁判同样对所有的球回后场违例负主要责任。有时当球在弱侧回场之前时，中央裁判同样可以协助判罚可能的球回后场违例。

2.19 进攻计时钟的区域分工

通常外侧的裁判员（追踪裁判和中央裁判）对进攻时间违例负主要责任。同时前导裁判也应注意进攻计时钟上的时间以便随时协助追踪裁判/中央裁判的判罚。裁判员了解什么时候进攻周期临近结束并随之做出正确的进攻时间违例的判罚是至关重要的。

所有情况下，管理掷球入界的执行裁判应检查进攻计时钟是否显示正确的时间，并且须在将球交于掷球入界队员前完成此程序。

注意：当篮板上沿装有黄色光带时，光带信号亮先于进攻计时钟信号响。

2.20 BASKET INTERFERENCE & GOALTENDING

Normally the Trail or Centre referee is responsible to determine if a basket interference or goaltending violation occurs. The referee opposite the shot has the primary responsibility for the flight of the ball and goaltending / basket interference violations. See also Diagram 56 & Diagram 57.

If a basket is awarded due to basket interference or goaltending the calling referee shall stop the clock and count the goal by showing the correct official signal.

Basket interference & goaltending on a fast break

In fast break situations it is primarily Centre´s and secondarily Lead's responsibility to cover the possible basket interference or goaltending violation. If the Centre is not ready to cover the fast break (physically not engaged with the play) the Lead could stop ahead of the endline to be able to see the ring and front of the backboard.

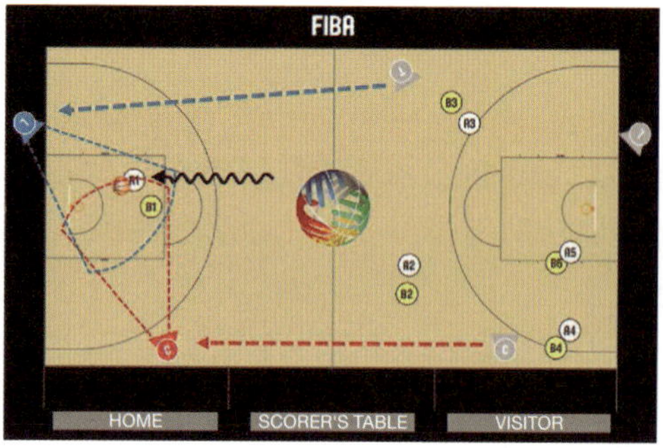

Diagram 45:
Normally in fast break situations Centre is responsible for basket interference or goaltending violations.

Basket interference & goaltending on a foul play

On all plays resulting in a foul call the Trail and Centre should not relax after the call. Instead they should hold their position, maintain their focus and follow the situation until the end (when the ball no longer has possibility to enter the basket) and be ready to make possible BI / GT call.

2.20 干扰得分与干涉得分

通常追踪裁判或中央裁判负责判罚是否发生一起干扰得分或干涉得分。投篮对侧的裁判员要对监控球的飞行以及干扰得分 / 干涉得分违例负主要责任。见图 56，图 57。

如果判给得分是因为干扰得分或干涉得分违例，宣判的裁判员应先停止比赛计时钟，随后用官方的手势来表示应计得分有效。

一次快攻情况中的干扰得分与干涉得分

在快攻情况中，中央裁判对监控有可能出现的干涉得分或干扰得分违例负有主要责任，追踪裁判负有次要责任。如果中央裁判没有准备好去监控快攻（由于身体原因没有跟上比赛），那么这就变成前导裁判的责任了。在这种情况下，前导裁判应当停步在端线前，尽可能看到篮圈和篮板的正面。

图 45：
在快攻情况中，通常中央裁判对发生干扰得分或干涉得分违例负责

犯规中的干涉得分和干扰得分违例

在裁判员吹罚了犯规之后，追踪裁判和中央裁判不应该放松，反而应该在这起情况结束（当球不再有可能进入球篮）之前保持他们的位置和注意力，并做好准备宣判有可能出现的干涉得分或干扰得分违例。

2.21 REPORTING FOULS & SWITCHING

Target: To identify and know the correct positions and procedures after a foul is called.

Principle for the switches:

Free throws (ball remains in the frontcourt):

a. Referee who reports the foul, moves to the opposite side in T position

b. Other 2 fill up the empty spots

Throw-in (ball remains in the frontcourt):

a. Referee who reports the foul, moves to the opposite side in T or C position

b. Other 2 fill up the empty spots

Minimize distance – walk sharp – think where is your next position after reporting. If two referees call the same foul, the referee who is on the opposite side will report the foul.

In all situations referees should try to minimize switches. Sometimes there is no switching needed, sometimes all three referees need to move in order for the above rules to be implemented.

Reporting:

a. Use clear voice

b. Sharp signals

c. Rhythm

See also "*2.8.1. Reporting*" in FIBA Referee Manual –Individual Officiating Techniques (IOT) for reporting technique and procedures.

2.21.1 BASIC SWITCHES

Below you find the switches explained in some of the basic foul situations. At the end of this manual in "*3.2 Switches after foul calls*" you can find more comprehensive list of examples.

2.21 报告犯规与换位

目标：明确和理解吹罚一起犯规后正确的落位与程序。

换位的原则：

罚球（球仍位于前场）：

a. 向记录台报号的裁判员，移动到记录台对侧 T 的位置

b. 另外两名裁判员填补其余空位

掷球入界（球仍位于前场）：

a. 向记录台报号的裁判员，移动到记录台对侧 T 或 C 的位置

b. 另外两名裁判填员补其余空位

最短的距离—快步走—思考报号后移动的下一个位置。如果两名裁判员同时对一起犯规吹哨，那么由位于记录台对侧的裁判员宣判这个犯规。

在所有情况下，裁判员应该尽量减少换位，为了实施以下的规则，有时裁判员无需换位，有时三名裁判员都需要移动位置。

报告犯规：

a. 声音清楚洪亮

b. 手势简单有力

c. 节奏清晰明了

更多报告犯规的技术与程序参见国际篮联裁判员手册中“2.8.1 报告犯规”——个人执裁技术。

2.21.1 基本换位

以下是一些基本犯规情况下的换位解析。在本手册末尾的“3.2 宣判犯规后的换位”中，你可以找到更全面的、更详细的举例列表。

Play remains in frontcourt, continued by throw-in

Diagram 46:
Defensive foul, frontcourt opposite side by L – ball remains in the frontcourt (throw-in)

Diagram 47:
Defensive foul, frontcourt opposite side by T – ball remains in the frontcourt (throw-in)

Diagram 48:
Defensive foul, frontcourt opposite side by C – ball remains in the frontcourt (throw-in)

Diagram 49:
Defensive foul, frontcourt table side by L – ball remains in the frontcourt (free throws)

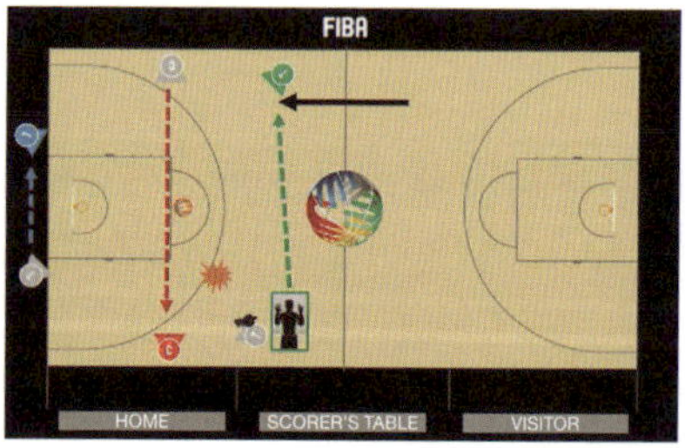

Diagram 50:
Defensive foul, frontcourt table side by T – ball remains in the frontcourt (free throws)

Diagram 51:
Call frontcourt table side by C – ball remains in the frontcourt (free throws)

球仍留在前场，随后以掷球入界恢复比赛

图 46：
防守犯规，L 位于前场记录台对侧——球仍留在前场（掷球入界）

图 47：
防守犯规，T 位于前场记录台对侧——球保持在前场（掷球入界）

图 48：
防守犯规，前场记录台对侧，C 鸣哨——球保持在前场（掷球入界）

图 49：
防守犯规，前场记录台同侧，L 鸣哨——球保持在前场（罚球）

图 50：
防守犯规，前场记录台同侧，T 鸣哨——球仍位于前场（罚球）

图 51：
前场记录台同侧，C 鸣哨——球保持在前场（罚球）

Play continues from new backcourt by throw-in

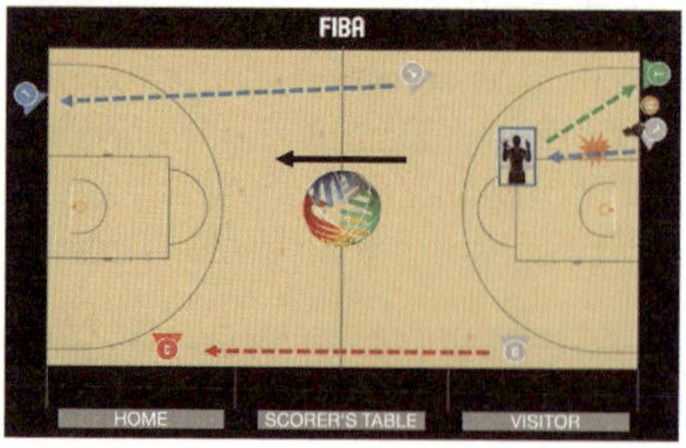

Diagram 52:
Call backcourt opposite side by L – ball moves new direction (throw-in)

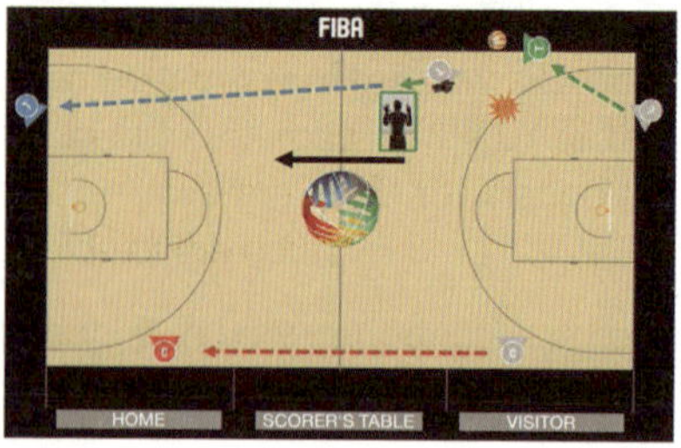

Diagram 53:
Call backcourt opposite side by T – ball moves new direction (throw-in)

2.22 FREE THROW COVERAGE

Target: To understand coverage and responsibilities during free throw situations and on following rebound plays.

In 3PO the Lead is the active referee in all free throw situations. Lead will administer all the free throws.During last free throw Lead is responsible for the players in rebound places on table side of the restricted area. For the last free-throw, the Lead should be positioned in the normal Lead set up position.

Centre indicates the number of free-throws using the official signals. On the all free throws, Centre is responsible for checking that there is no violation from the shooter. During last free throw Centre is responsible for the players in rebound places on opposite side of the restricted area. During the freethrows, the Centre is to be positioned near the side line in the normal Centre position.

Trail is responsible for the rest of the players behind the free-throw line extended and behind the 3-point line during all free throws.

When a violation occurs during the free throw and the ball is in the air, the referee should immediately blow the whistle to indicate the violation (exception: fake by free-throw shooter). This is to minimize any unnecessary escalation of physical contact between players after a violation occurs. There is no need to wait if the ball enters the basket or not.

罚球后从新的后场掷球入界继续比赛

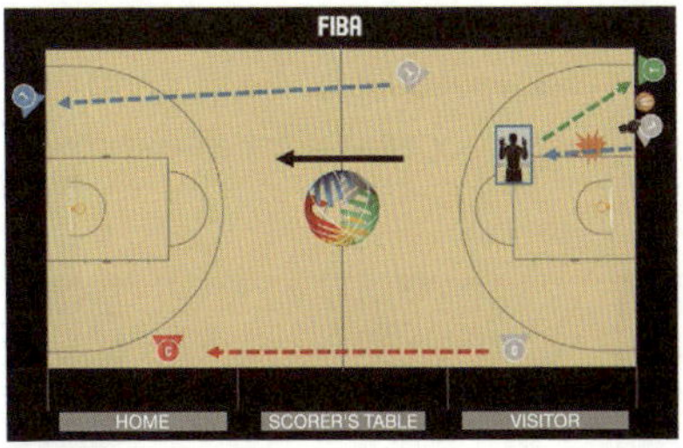

图 52：
后场记录台对侧，L 鸣哨——球移动到新的方向（掷球入界）

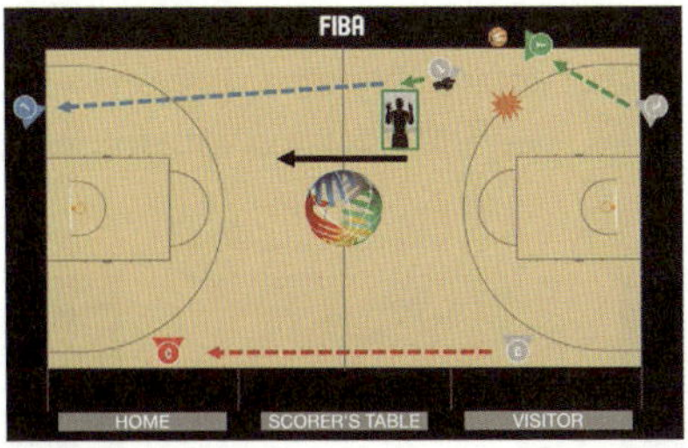

图 53：
后场记录台对侧，T 鸣哨——球移动到新的方向（掷球入界）

2.22 罚球的区域分工

目标：理解罚球期间的视野覆盖和责任分工以及后续的篮板球情况。

3 人执裁时，前导裁判在所有的罚球情况中都是执行裁判。前导裁判要管理所有的罚球。在最后一次罚球中，前导裁判要负责观察位于记录台侧限制区边缘的分位区内的队员。对于最后一次罚球，前导裁判应位于通常情况下的初始位置。

中央裁判做出指示罚球次数的官方手势。所有的罚球情况中，中央裁判负责观察是否出现罚球队员的违例。中央裁判负责观察位于对侧限制区边缘的分位区内的队员。在罚球中，中央裁判应位于靠近边线处通常情况下的初始位置。

在罚球期间，追踪裁判负责罚球线延长线后 3 分线外的其余的队员。

当罚球期间发生一起违例并且球在空中时，裁判员应立即鸣哨并指明违例情况（例如：罚球队员假动作）。这是为了减少违例发生后队员之间不必要的身体接触。没有必要等到球是否进入球篮。

If the ball enters the basket:

a. violation by free-throw shooter - basket is not valid

b. violation by other players – basket is valid, whistle is to be ignored and play will continue with throw-in as after any successful last free-throw.

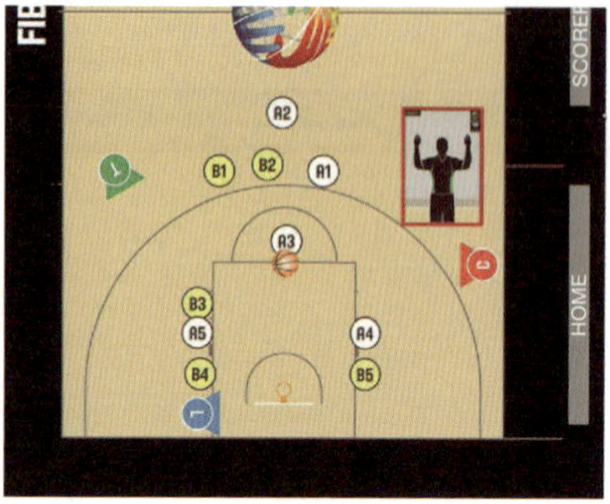

Diagram 54:
Only Centre indicates the number of free throws using the official signals.

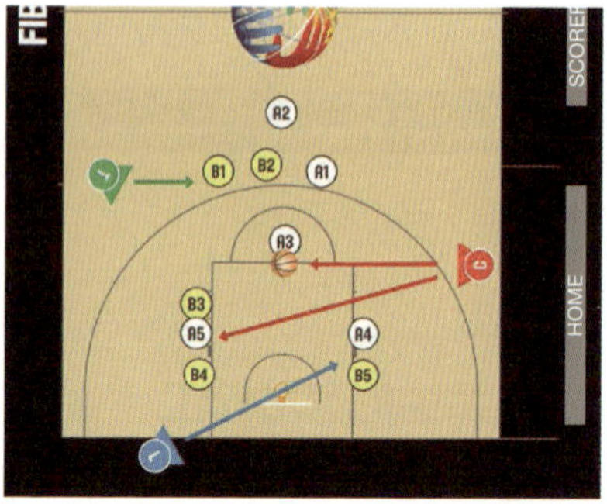

Diagram 55:
Primary responsibilities during last or only free throw.

2.23 REBOUNDING COVERAGE

Target: To identify the correct techniques for total coverage during rebounding situations to ensure that not more than 1-2 active match-ups are covered by each referee.

In rebounding situations each referee should pick up 1-2 active match ups the moment a shot has been attempted. Generally best way is to pick up those closest to you. Use the pre-game conference to discuss the correct plan, methods and execution.

Shot from the strong side: Lead covers the match-up close to the basket (holding and clamping fouls), Trail & Centre focus on perimeter rebounds (pushing, crashing and "over-the-back") on their respective sides. Centre has primary coverage on goaltending or basket interference as Trail has shot coverage (Diagram 56).

如果球进入了球篮：

a. 罚球队员违例——中篮应不计得分

b. 其他任意队员违例——中篮应计得分，鸣哨应被忽略，随后应如同最后一次罚球成功以掷球入界恢复比赛。

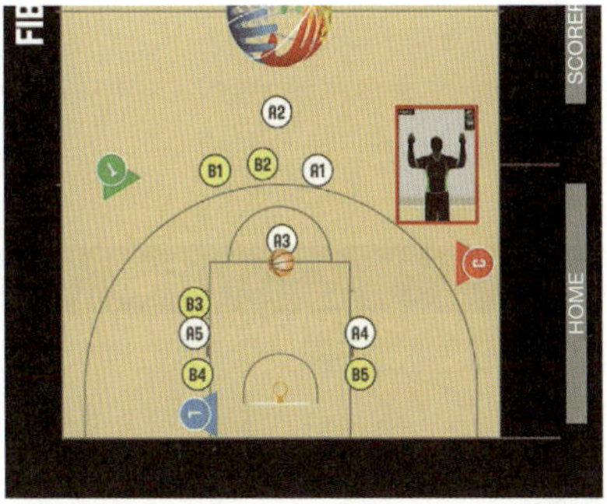

图 54：
只有中央裁判做出指示罚球次数的官方手势

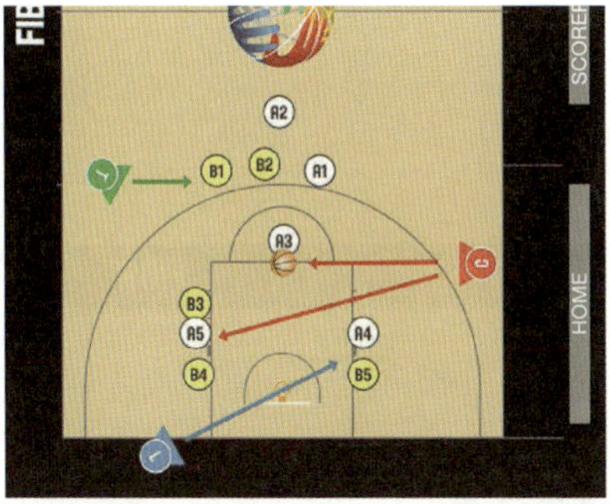

图 55：
在最后一次罚球或仅有一次罚球时，裁判员的责任分工

2.23 篮板球的区域分工

目标：明确篮板球情况中整体区域分工配合的正确技巧，确保每名裁判员只需负责观察 1~2 对位。

在投篮出手瞬间的篮板球情况中每一名裁判员应该只监控 1~2 个对位矛盾，一般来说最好的方法就是监控离你最近的。利用赛前准备会来讨论正确的计划、方法和执行策略。

强侧的投篮：前导裁判负责监控靠近球篮的对位（拉人和夹人的犯规），追踪裁判和中央裁判监控各自区域的外围篮板球（推人、撞人以及压肩背）。当追踪裁判监控投篮时，中央裁判主要负责监控干扰得分和干涉得分。（图 56）

Shot from the weak side: Lead covers the match-up close to basket (holding and clamping fouls), Trail & Centre focus on perimeter rebounds (pushing, crashing and "over-the-back") on their respective sides. Trail has primary coverage on goaltending or basket interference as Centre has shot coverage (Diagram 57).

If there are no active match-ups on your side, you need to move to the next active match-up! (not engaged with mechanics but the play & active mind-set)

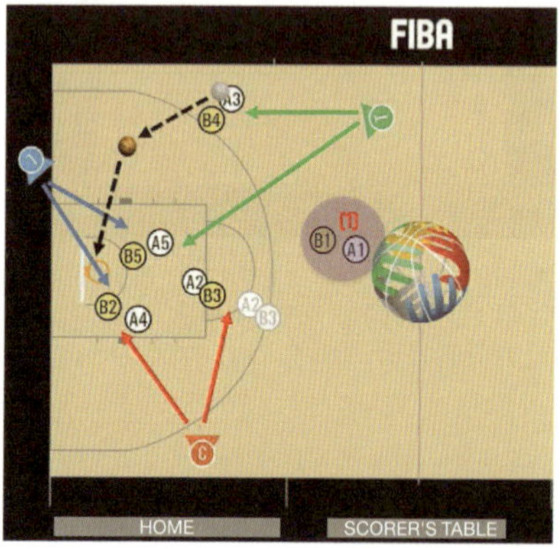

Diagram 56:
Shot from the strong side, L focus on players close to basket, T & C focus on perimeter players and C has the primary for the possible goaltending and basket interference. (1) = not active match–up.

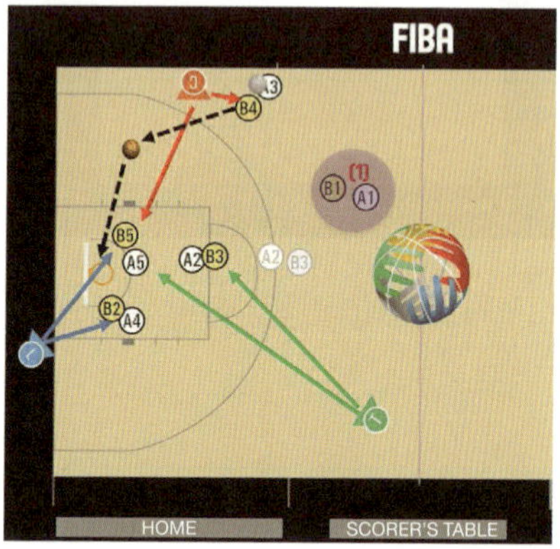

Diagram 57:
Shot from the weak side, L focus on players close to basket, T & C focus on perimeter players and T has the primary for the possible goaltending and basket interference. (1) = not active match–up.

弱侧的投篮：前导裁判负责监控靠近球篮的对位（拉人或夹人的犯规），追踪裁判和中央裁判监控各自区域的外围篮板球（推人、撞人以及压肩背）。当中央裁判监控投篮时，追踪裁判主要负责监控干扰得分和干涉得分。（图 57）

如果你的一侧的对位没有矛盾，
你需要将视线转移到有矛盾的对位上！
（不要机械地执裁，应顺应比赛并保持动态思维）

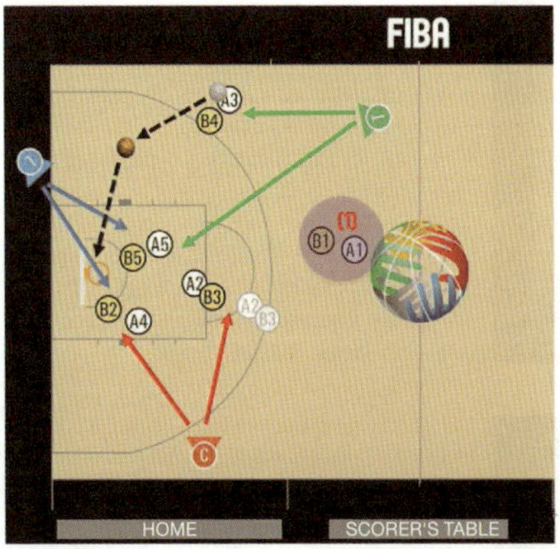

图 56：
强侧的投篮，L 监控靠近球篮的队员，T 和 C 监控外围的队员，C 主要负责监控可能出现的干扰得分和干涉得分 [1]= 没有矛盾的对位

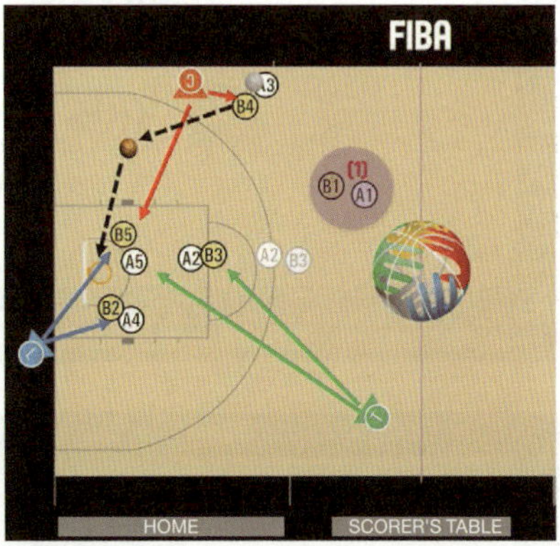

图 57：
弱侧的投篮，L 监控靠近球篮的队员，T 和 C 监控外围的队员，T 主要负责监控可能出现的干扰得分和干涉得分 [1]= 没有矛盾的对位

2.24 LAST SHOT

Target: To identify which referee is on the last shot and who is responsible for controlling the game/shot clock at the end of a quarter or the game.

Normally, either the Trail or Centre decide if any shot close to the end of a quarter or game is a valid basket or if the ball was not released before the LED light/signal.

Diagram 58:
Last shot on opposite side:

- the Trail or Centre on table side (Trail or Centre) is primarily responsible for the clock (primary mode)
- the Trail or Centre (who is covering the shooting situation) on opposite side is secondarily responsible for the clock (assist mode)

Diagram 59:
Last shot on table side:

- the Trail or Centre on opposite side (Trail or Centre) is primarily responsible for the clock (primary mode)
- the Trail or Centre (who is covering the shooting situation) on table side is secondarily responsible for the clock (assist mode)

If any of the referees not covering the last shot have information regarding the last shot and the clock, they are required to go immediately to the calling referee who is responsible for the last shot and share this information with the crew (assist mode).

In the event there is disagreement amongst the crew, the Crew Chief always makes the final decision.

2.24 最后一投

目标：确认一节比赛或全场比赛的最后时刻，在最后一投中，哪名裁判员负责监控投篮，以及哪名裁判员负责控制比赛 / 进攻计时钟

通常情况下由追踪裁判或中央裁判来决定临近一节比赛或全场比赛结束时的投篮是否有效，或者在 LED 灯亮 / 信号响之前球是否离开队员的手。

图 58：
最后一投发生在记录台对侧：
- 记录台侧的 T 或 C 对计时钟负主要责任（主责）
- 对侧的 T 或 C（正在观察投篮情况）对计时钟负次要责任（协助）

图 59：
最后一投发生在记录台侧：
- 对侧的 T 或 C 对计时钟负主要责任（主责）
- 记录台侧的 T 或 C（正在观察投篮情况）对计时钟负次要责任（协助）

如果其他无需观察投篮情况的裁判员掌握了与最后一投以及计时钟相关的信息，他们应立即与负责宣判最后一投的裁判员商讨，并且与整个裁判组分享相关信息（协助）。

当裁判员之间存在意见分歧时，主裁判负责做出最终判罚。

第3章

SUPPORTING MATERIAL

支撑资料

CHAPTER 3

3. SUPPORTING MATERIAL

3.1 OFFICIAL REFEREES' SIGNALS

Game clock signals

STOP THE CLOCK

Open palm

STOP THE CLOCK FOR FOUL

One clenched fist

START THE CLOCK

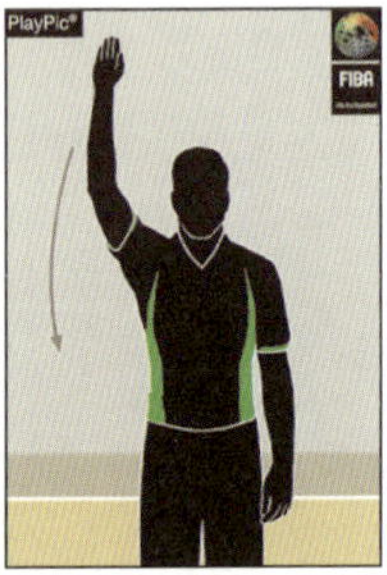

Chop with hand

Scoring

1 POINT

1 finger,
'flag' from wrist

2 POINTS

2 fingers,
'flag' from wrist

3 POINTS

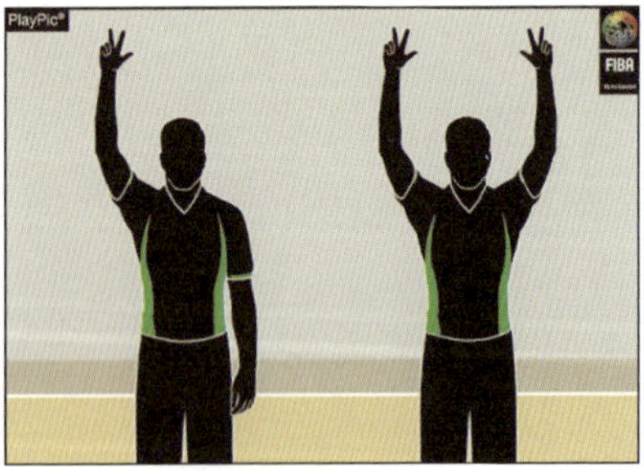

3 fingers extended
One arm: Attempt
Both arms: Successful

第 3 章

3. 支撑资料

3.1 官方裁判员手势

比赛计时钟信号

停止计时钟

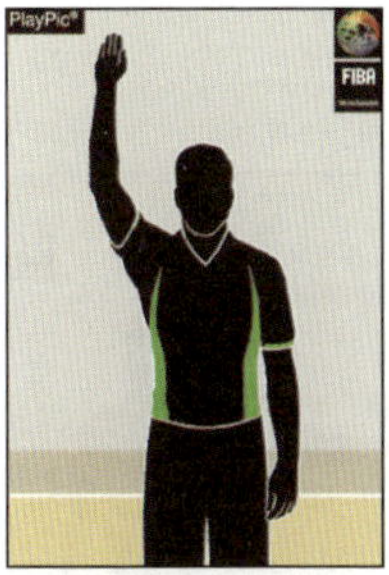

伸开手掌

犯规停止计时钟

一拳紧握

计时开始

用手做劈砍

得分

1 分

1 指
从腕部下屈

2 分

2 指
从腕部下屈

3 分

伸展 3 指
一只胳膊：3 分试投
两只胳膊：3 分投篮成功

Substitution and Time-out

SUBSTITUTION

Cross forearms

BECKONING-IN

Open palm, wave towards the body

CHARGED TIME-OUT

Form T, show index finger

MEDIA TIME-OUT

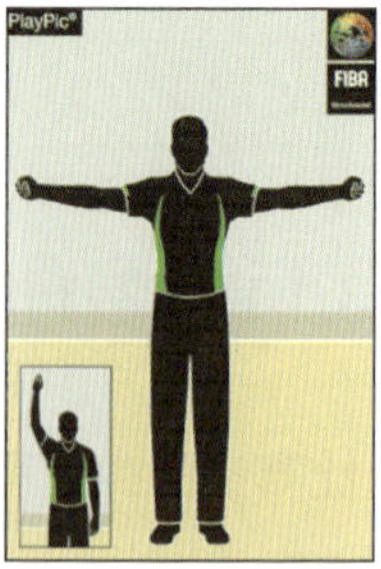

Open arms with clenched fists

Informative

CANCEL SCORE, CANCEL PLAY

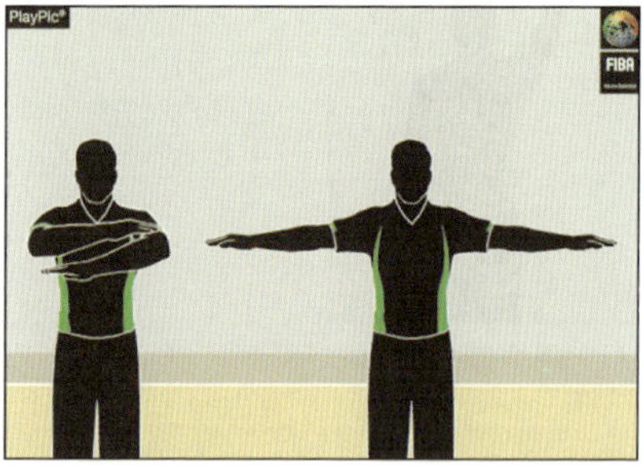

Scissor-like action with arms, once across chest

VISIBLE COUNT

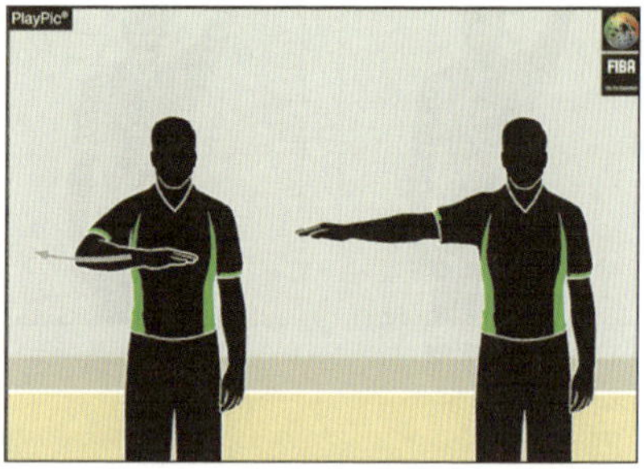

Counting while moving the palm

COMMUNICATION

Thumb up

SHOT CLOCK RESET

Rotate hand, extend index finger

DIRECTION OF PLAY AND/OR OUT-OF-BOUNDS

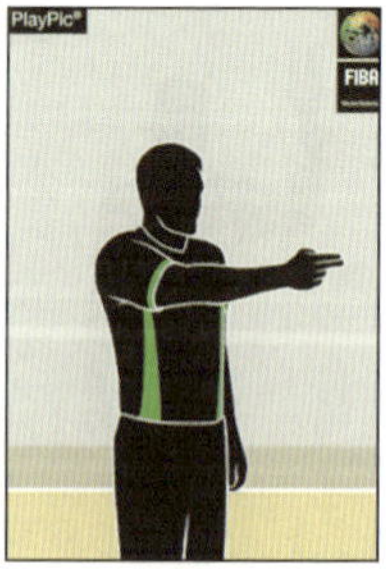

Point in direction of play, arm parallel to sidelines

HELD BALL/JUMP BALL SITUATION

Thumbs up, then point in direction of play using the alternating possession arrow

替换和暂停

替换

前臂交叉

招呼入场

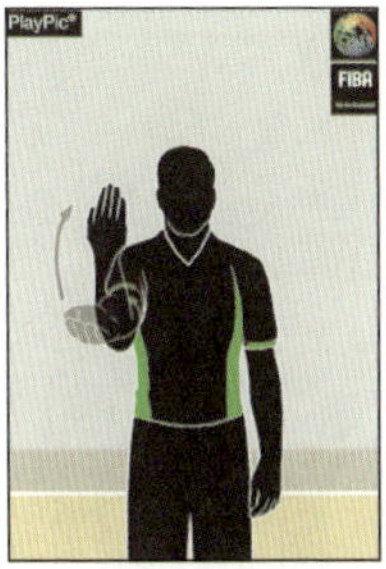

伸出手掌
摆向身体

暂停

成“T”形
食指示之

媒体暂停

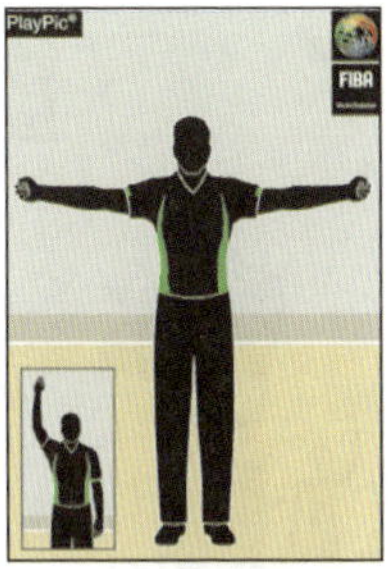

张开双臂
紧握拳头

提供信息

取消得分，中止比赛

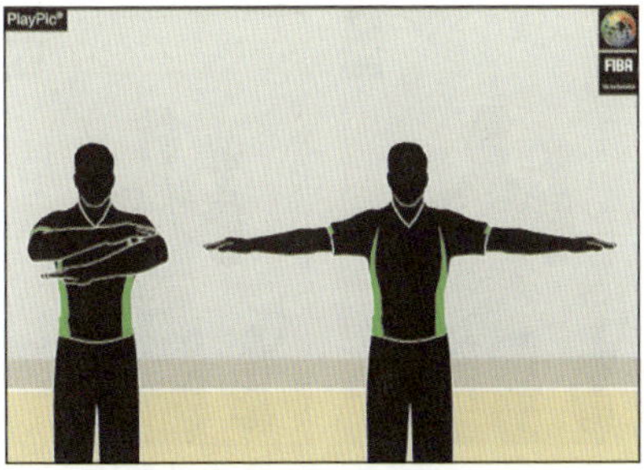

双臂像剪的动作，胸前交叉一次

可见的计数

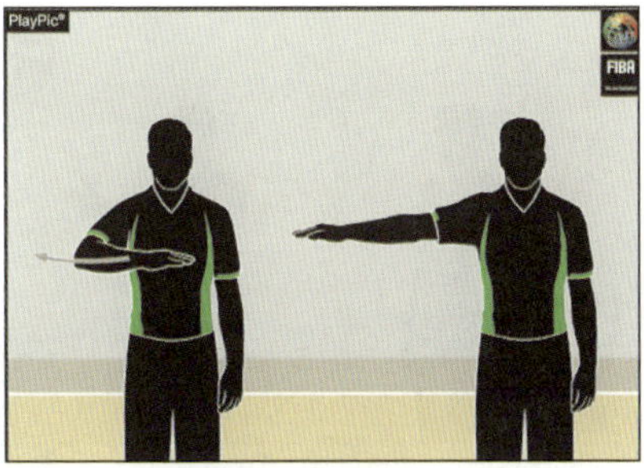

移动手掌计数

交流

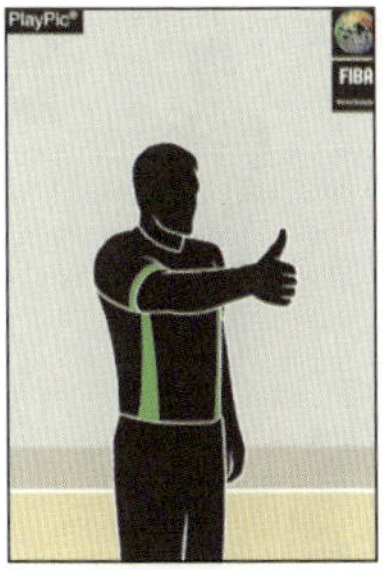

拇指向上

进攻计时钟复位

伸出食指
并转动手

比赛方向和 / 或出界

指向比赛方向，
手臂与边线平行

争球 / 跳球情况

两拇指向上，然后
指向交替拥有箭头
所指的比赛方向

Violations

TRAVELLING

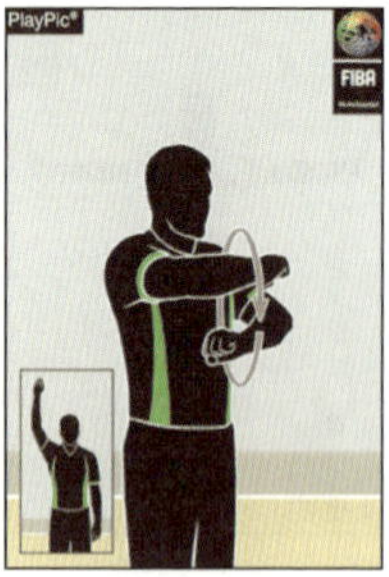

Rotate fists

ILLEGAL DRIBBLE: DOUBLE DRIBBLING

Patting motion with palm

ILLEGAL DRIBBLE: CARRYING THE BALL

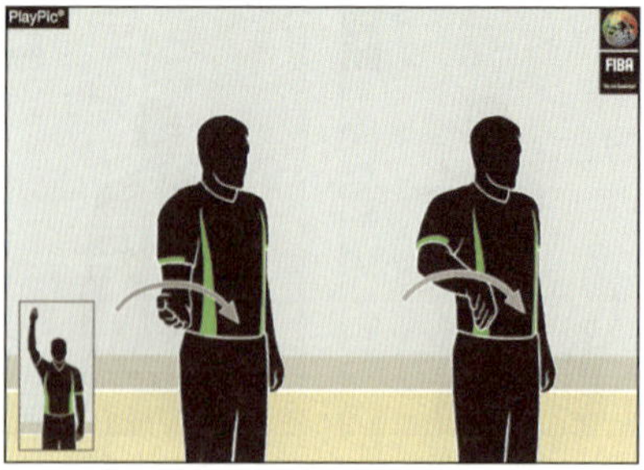

Half rotation with palm

3 SECONDS

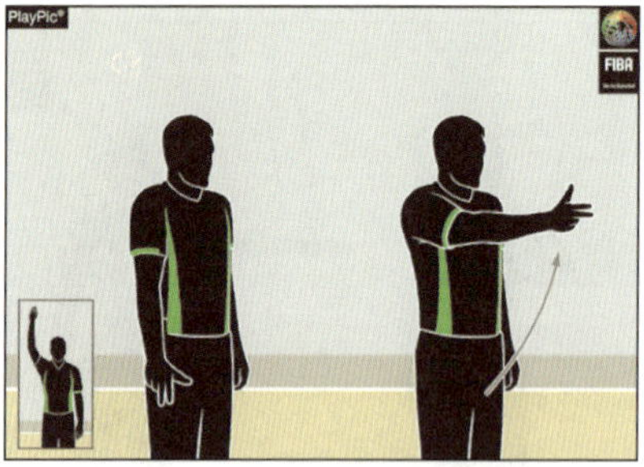

Arm extended, show 3 fingers

5 SECONDS

Show 5 fingers

8 SECONDS

Show 8 fingers

24 SECONDS

Fingers touch shoulder

BALL RETURNED TO BACKCOURT

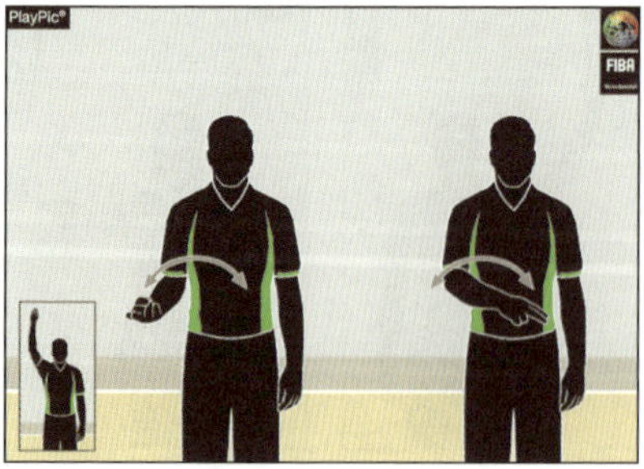

Wave arm front of body

DELIBERATE KICK OR BLOCK OF THE BALL

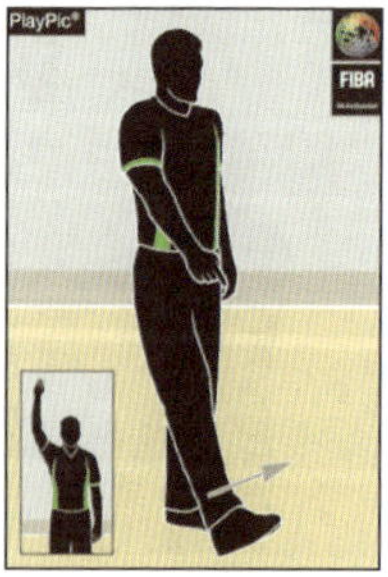

Point to the foot

违例

带球走

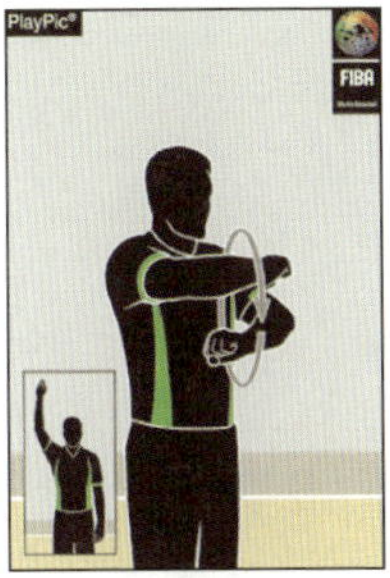

转动双拳

非法运球：两次运球

用手掌做轻拍动作

非法运球：携带球

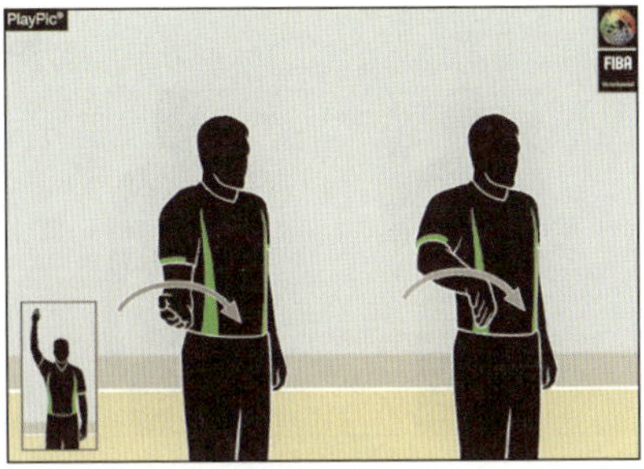

半转手掌

3 秒钟

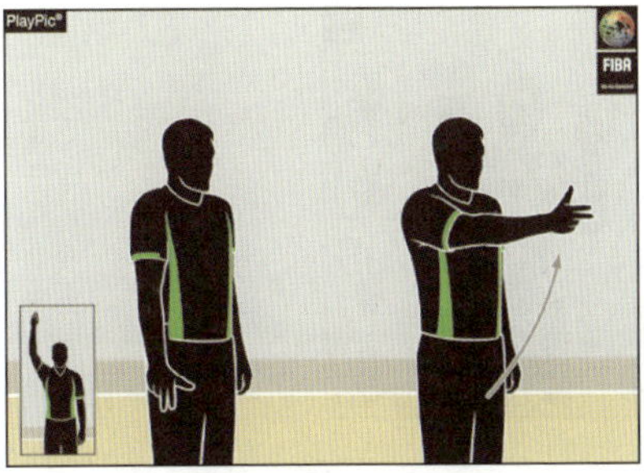

伸出手臂示 3 指

5 秒钟

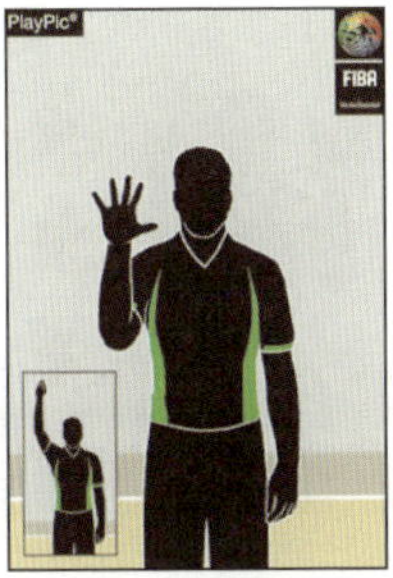

示 5 指

8 秒钟

示 8 指

24 秒钟

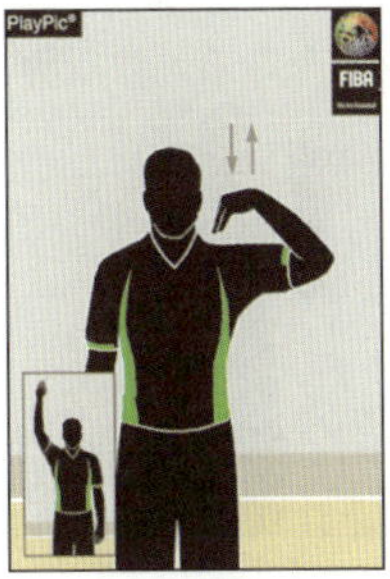

手指触肩

球回后场

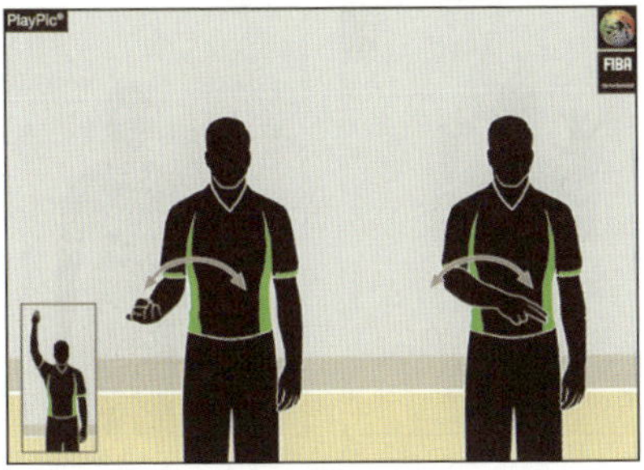

身前摆动手臂

故意脚踢或拦阻球

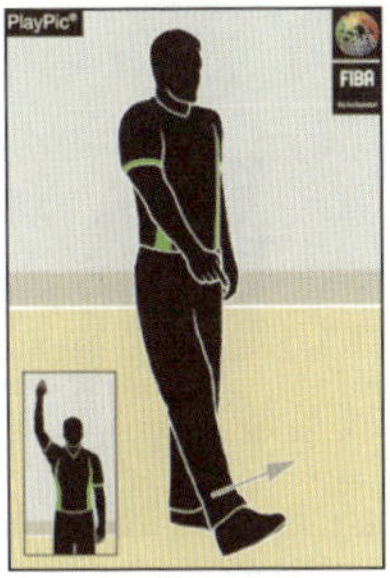

手指指脚

Number of Players

No. 00 and 0

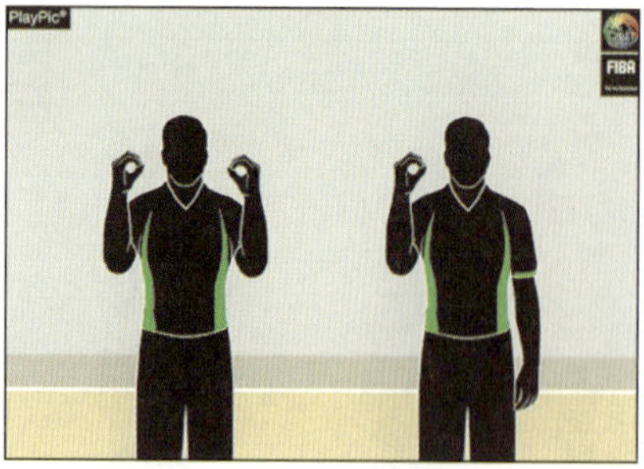

Both hands show number 0

Right hand shows number 0

No. 1 - 5

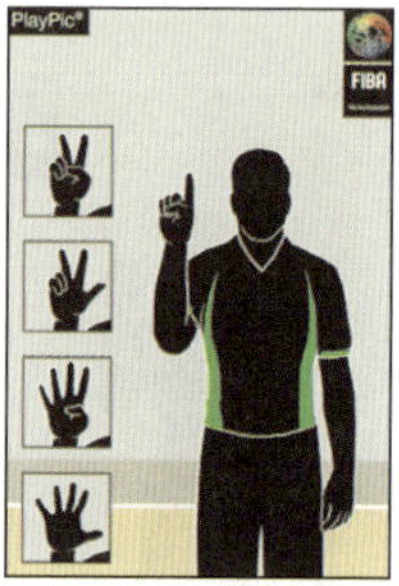

Right hand shows number 1 to 5

No. 6 - 10

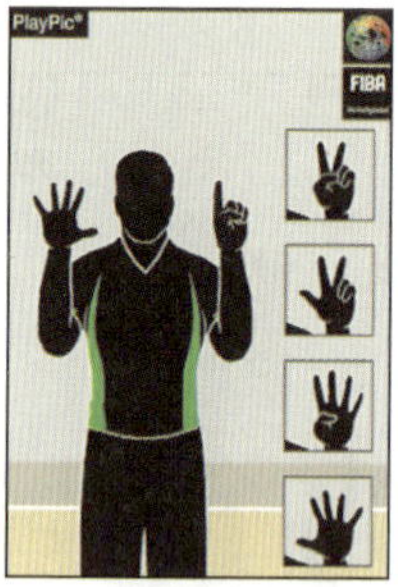

Right hand shows number 5, left hand shows number 1 to 5

No. 11 - 15

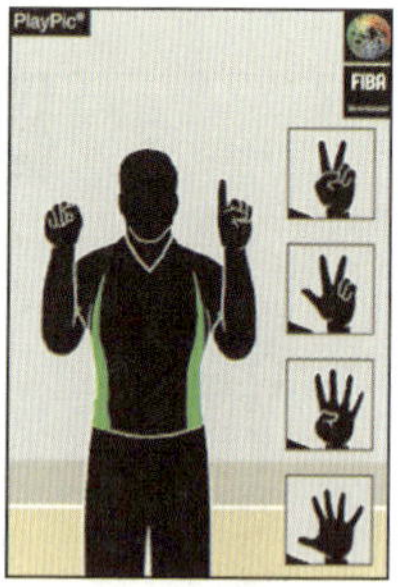

Right hand shows clenched fist, left hand shows number 1 to 5

No. 16

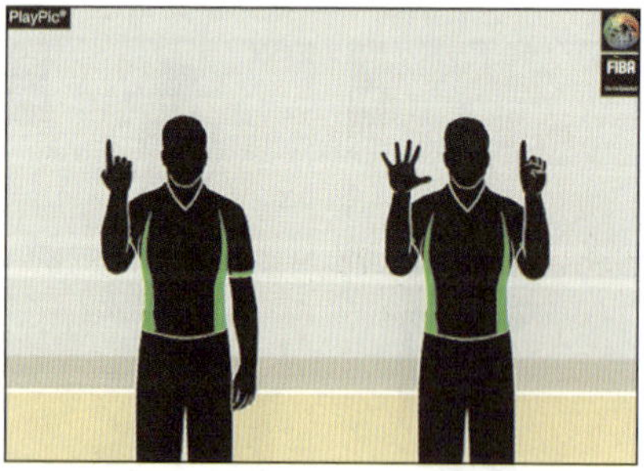

First reverse hand shows number 1 for the decade digit - then open hands show number 6 for the units digit

No. 24

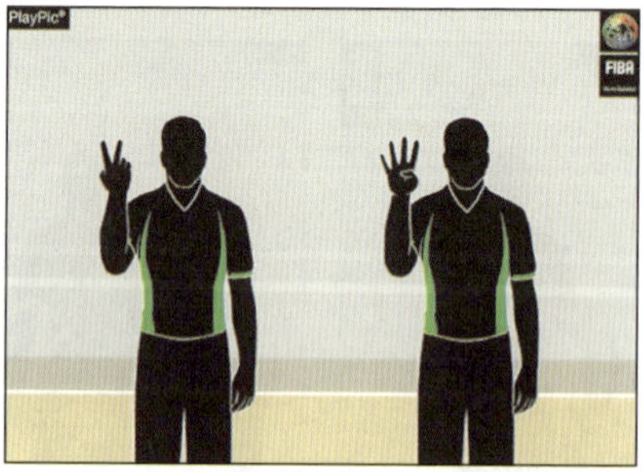

First reverse hand shows number 2 for the decade digit - then open hand shows number 4 for the units digit

队员的号码

No.00 和 No.0

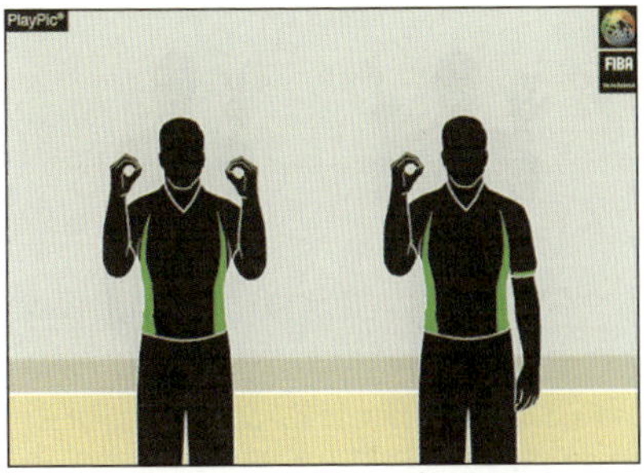

双手示 0 号　　右手示 0 号

No.1-5

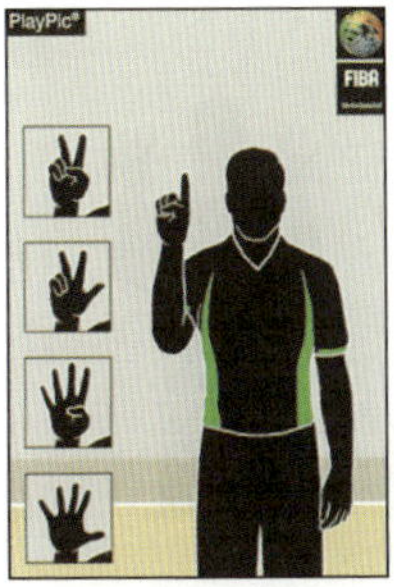

右手示号码 1 到 5

No.6-10

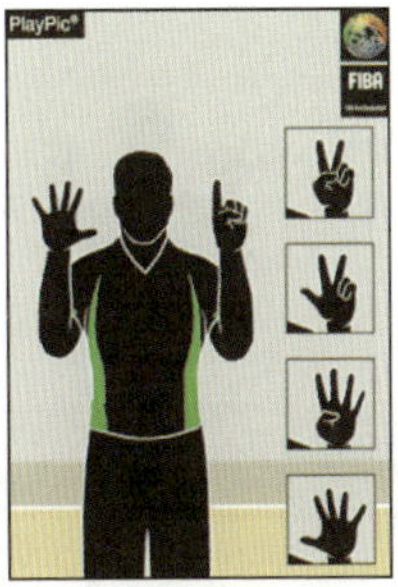

右手示 5 号，
左手示号码 1 到 5

No.11-15

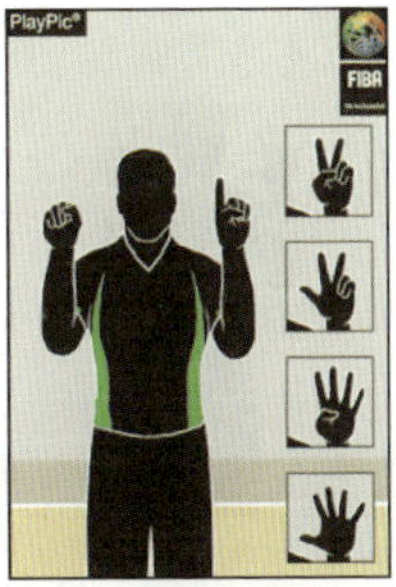

右手示紧握的拳头，
左手示号码 1 到 5

No.16

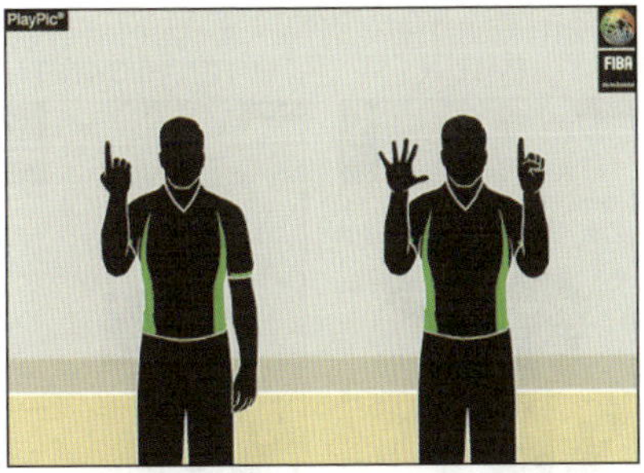

首先手背朝外示 1 号代表十位数，
然后手掌朝外示 6 号代表个位数

No.24

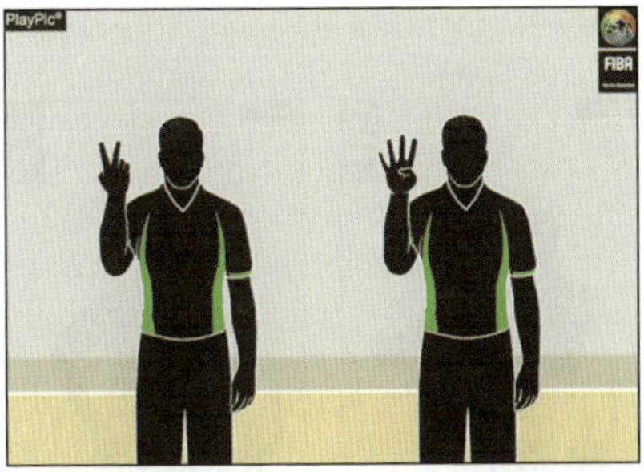

首先手背朝外示 2 号代表十位数，
然后手掌朝外示 4 号代表个位数

No. 40

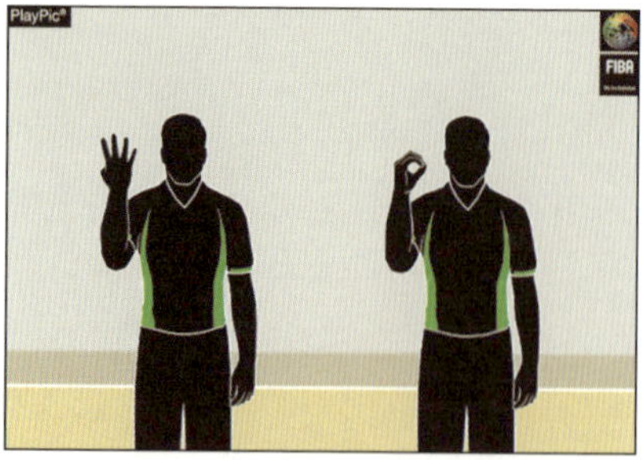

First reverse hand shows number 4 for the decade digit - then open hand shows number 0 for the units digit

No. 62

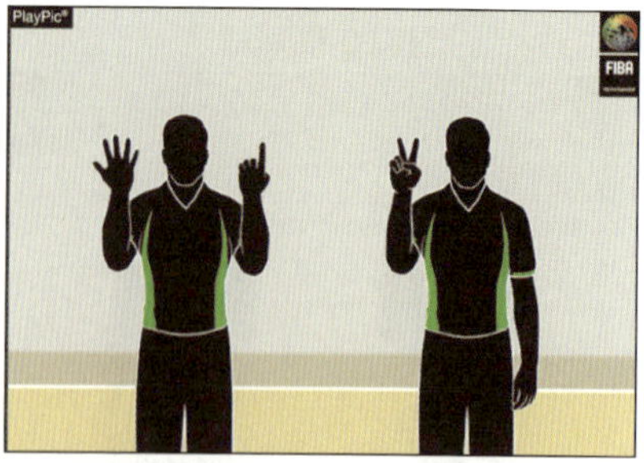

First reverse hands show number 6 for the decade digit - then open hand shows number 2 for the units digit

No. 78

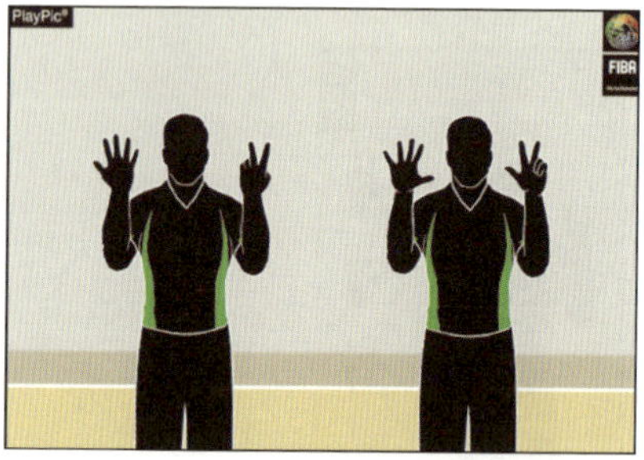

First reverse hands show number 7 for the decade digit - then open hands show number 8 for the units digit

No. 99

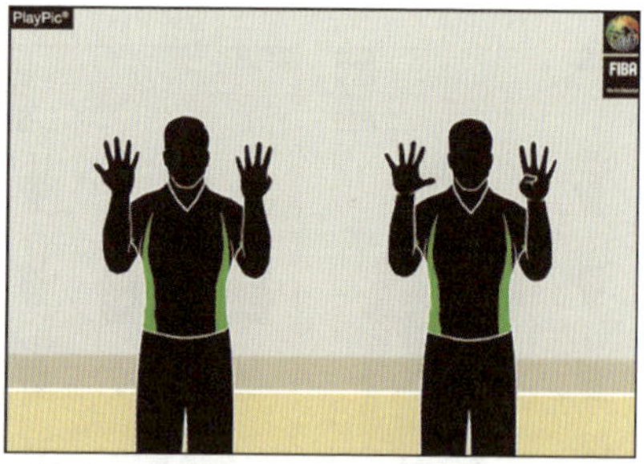

First reverse hands show number 9 for the decade digit - then open hands show number 9 for the units digit

Type of Fouls

HOLDING

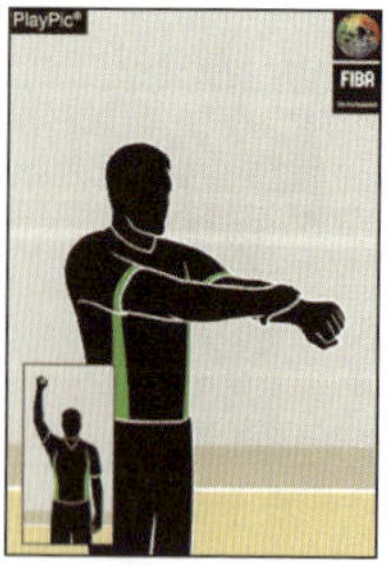

Grasp wrist downward

BLOCKING (DEFENSE), ILLEGAL SCREEN (OFFENSE)

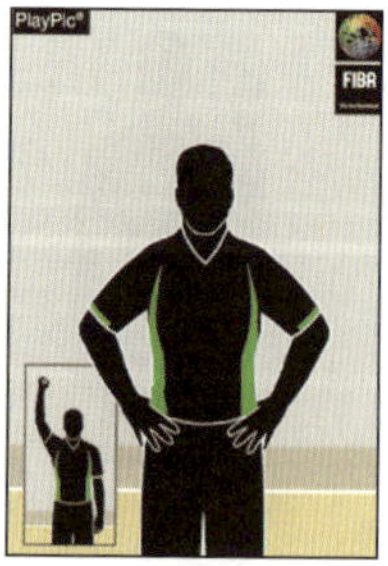

Both hands on hips

PUSHING OR CHARGING WITHOUT THE BALL

Imitate push

HANDCHECKING

Grab palm and forward motion

No.40

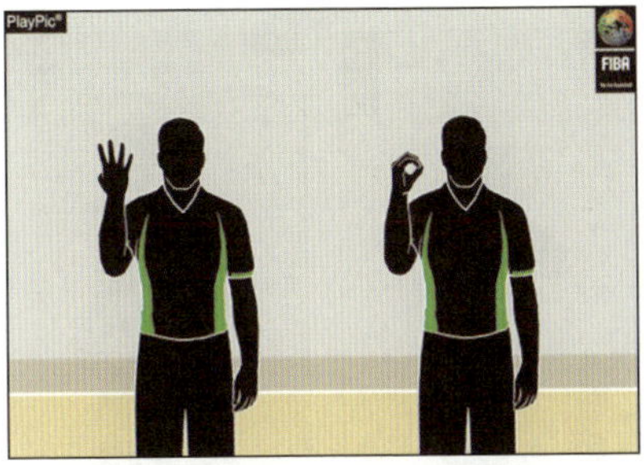

首先手背朝外示4号代表十位数，
然后手掌朝外示 0 号代表个位数

No.62

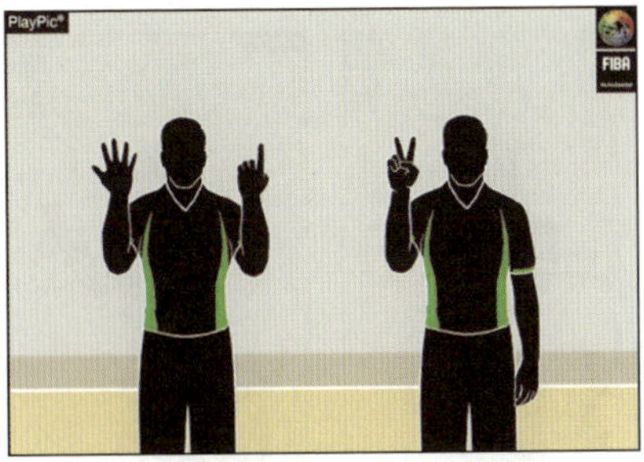

首先手背朝外示6号代表十位数，
然后手掌朝外示 2 号代表个位数

No.78

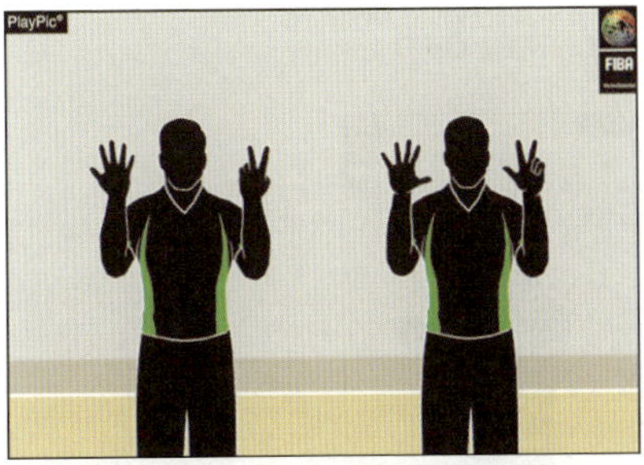

首先手背朝外示7号代表十位数，
然后手掌朝外示 8 号代表个位数

No.99

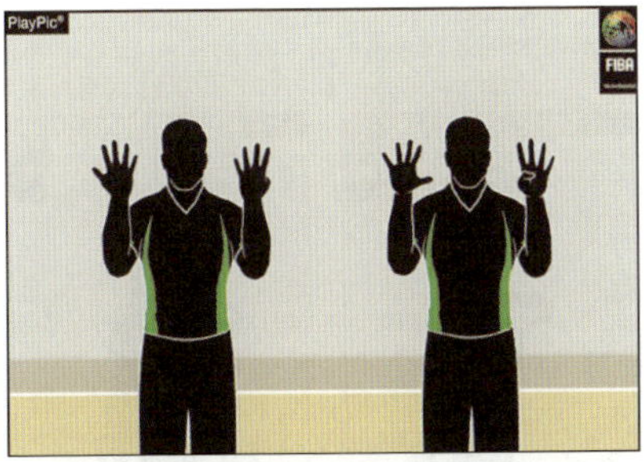

首先手背朝外示9号代表十位数，
然后手掌朝外示 9 号代表个位数

犯规的类型

拉人

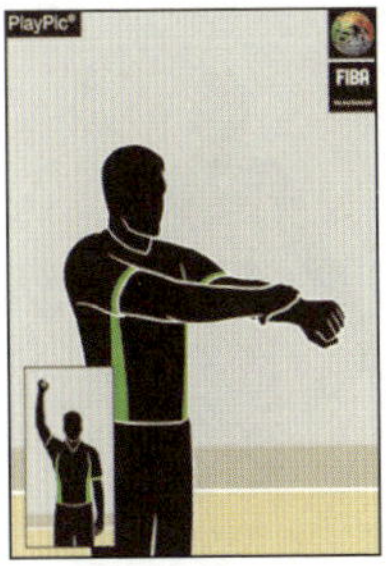

向下抓住手腕

阻挡（防守）
非法掩护（进攻）

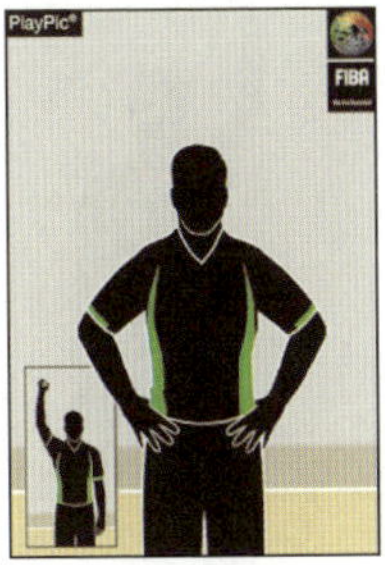

双手置髋部

推人或
不带球撞人

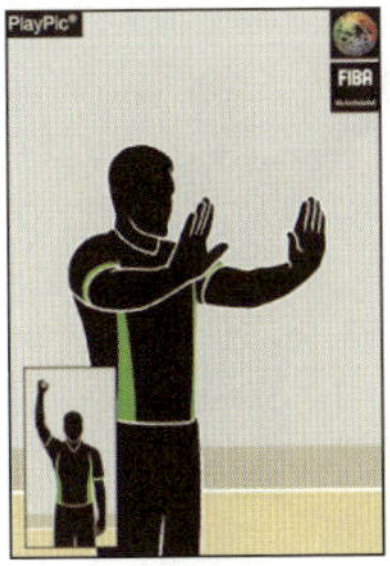

模仿推

用手推挡

抓住手掌向前移动

ILLEGAL USE OF HANDS

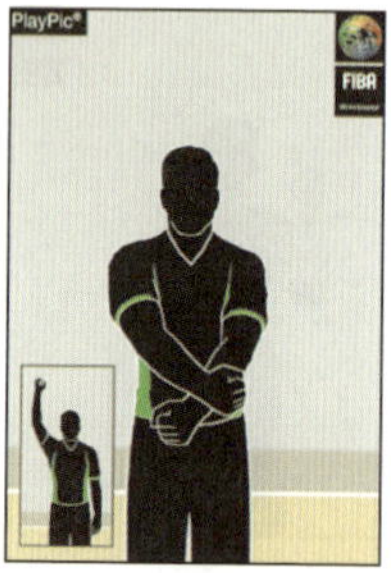

Strike wrist

CHARGING WITH THE BALL

Clenched fist strike open palm

ILLEGAL CONTACT TO THE HAND

Strike the palm towards the other forearm

HOOKING

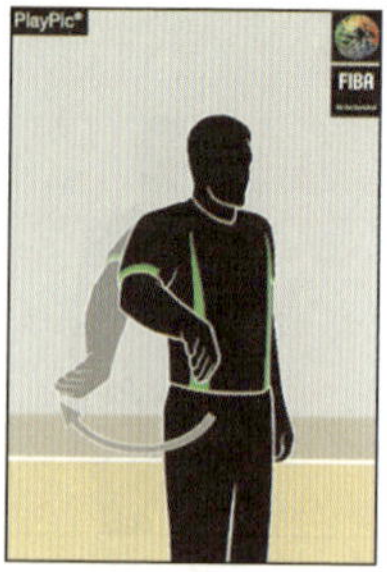

Move lower arm backwards

EXCESSIVE SWINGING OF ELBOW

Swing elbow backwards

HIT TO THE HEAD

Imitate the contact to the head

FOUL BY TEAM IN CONTROL OF THE BALL

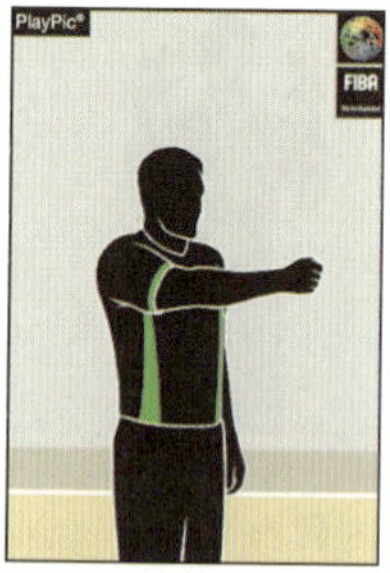

Point clenched fist towards basket of offending team

FOUL ON THE ACT OF SHOOTING

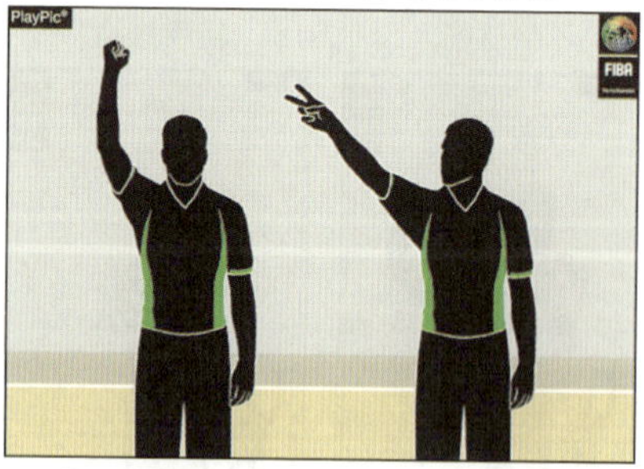

One arm with clenched fist, followed by indication of the number of free throws

FOUL NOT ON THE ACT OF SHOOTING

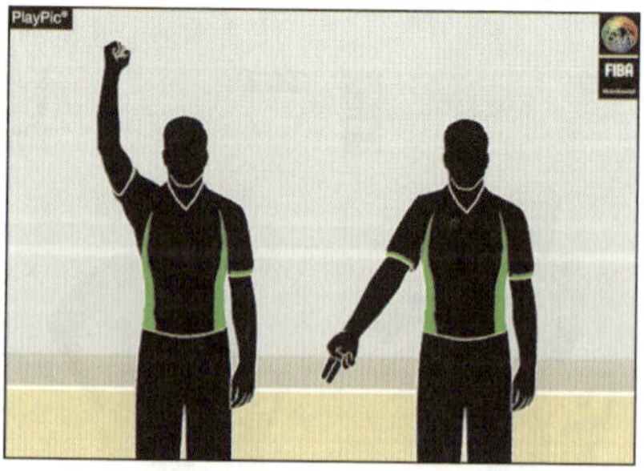

One arm with clenched fist, followed by pointing to the floor

非法用手

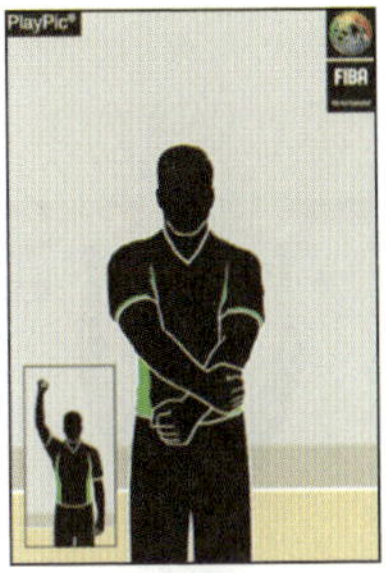

击腕

带球撞人

握拳击掌

对手的非法接触

掌击另一只前臂

勾人犯规

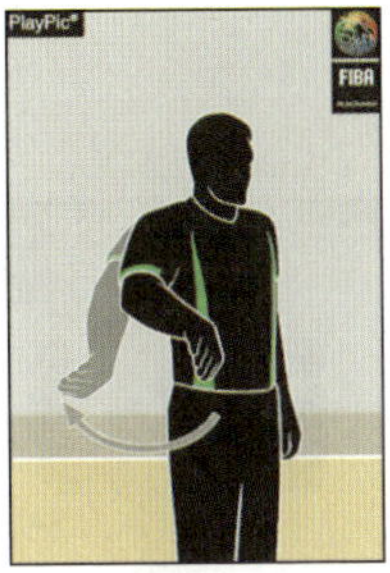

向后移动前臂

过分挥肘

向后摆肘

击头

模仿拍击头部

控制球队的犯规

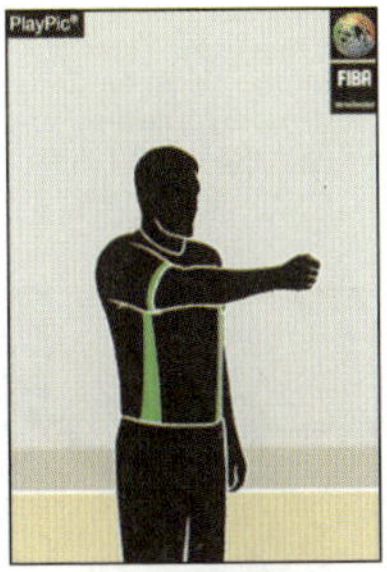

握拳指向犯规队的球篮

对投篮动作的犯规

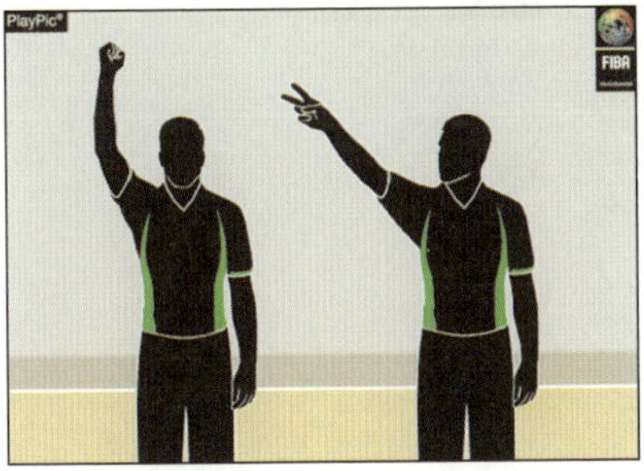

单臂握拳举起，随后指示罚球次数

对非投篮动作的犯规

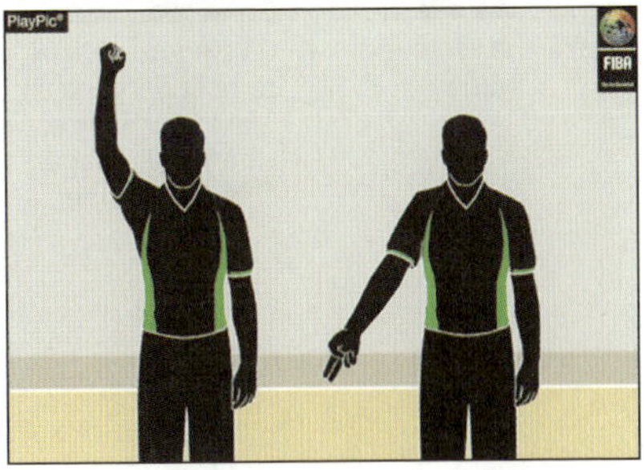

单臂握拳举起，随后指向地面

Special Fouls

DOUBLE FOUL

Wave clenched fists on both hands

TECHNICAL FOUL

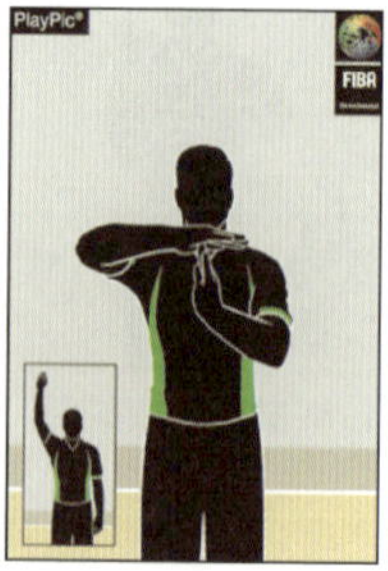

Form T, showing palms

UNSPORTSMANLIKE FOUL

Grasp wrist upward

DISQUALIFYING FOUL

Clenched fists on both hands

FAKE A FOUL

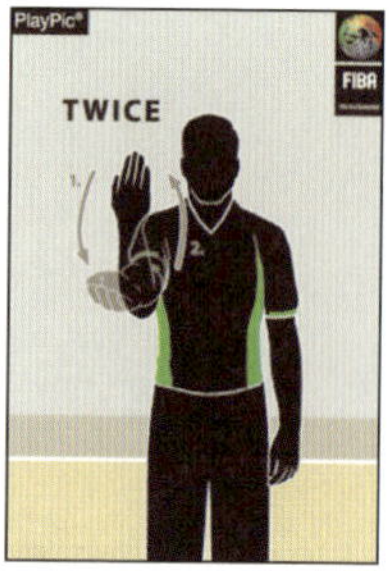

Raise the lower arm twice

ILLEGAL BOUNDARY LINE CROSSING ON A THROW-IN

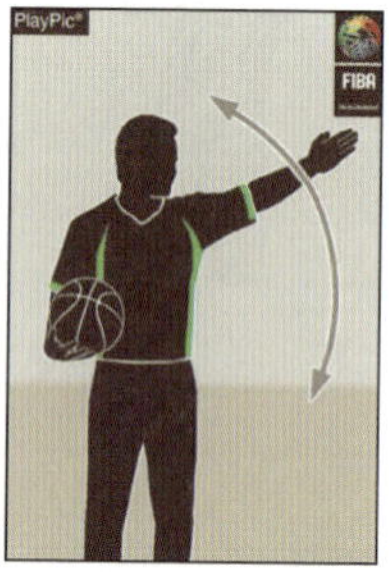

Wave arm parallel to boundary line (in last 2 minutes of the fourth quarter and overtime)

IRS REVIEW

Rotate hand with horizontal extended index finger

特殊犯规

双方犯规

挥动紧握的双拳

技术犯规

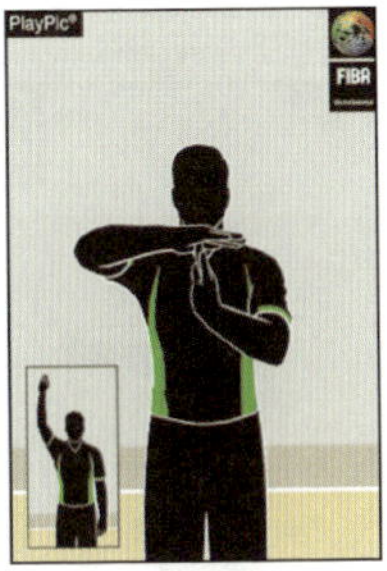

成“T”形手掌示之

违反体育运动精神的犯规

向上抓住手腕

取消比赛资格的犯规

紧握双拳

骗取犯规

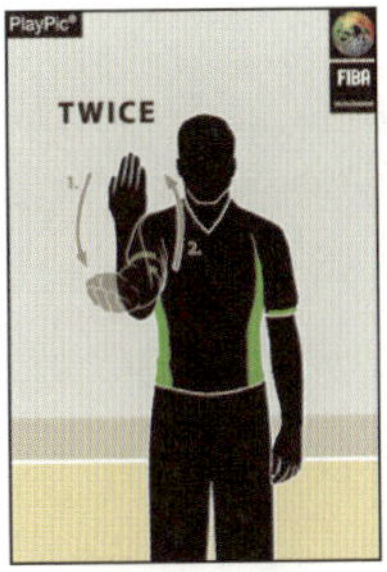

前臂上抬两次
（从高处做起）

掷球入界非法越线

平行于界线摆动手臂（第 4 节和决胜期最后 2 分钟）

调用即时回放系统

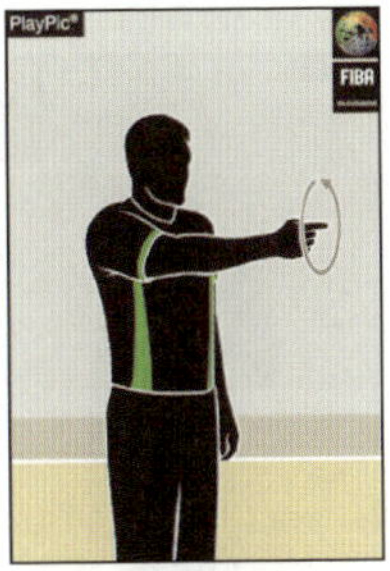

水平伸直食指
转动手

Foul Penalty Administration – Reporting to Table

AFTER FOUL WITHOUT FREE THROW(S)

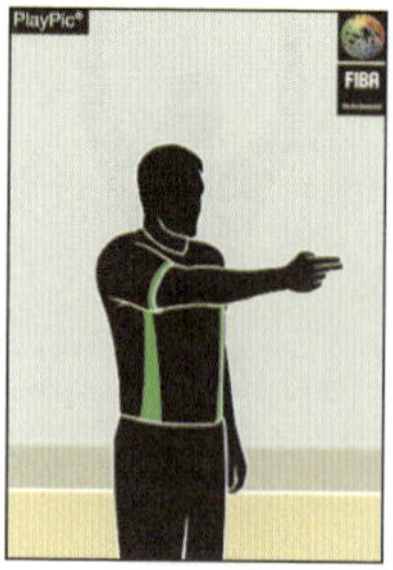

Point in direction of play, arm parallel to sidelines

AFTER FOUL BY TEAM IN CONTROL OF THE BALL

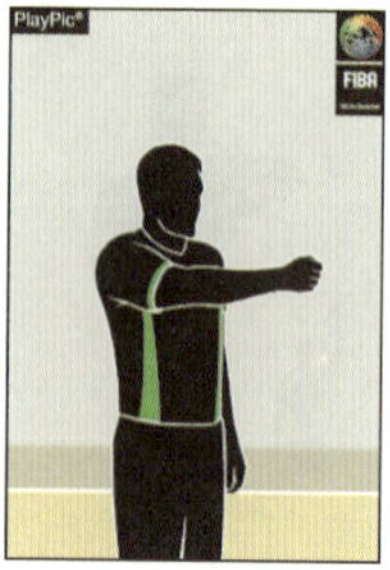

Clenched fist in direction of play, arm parallel to sidelines

1 FREE THROW

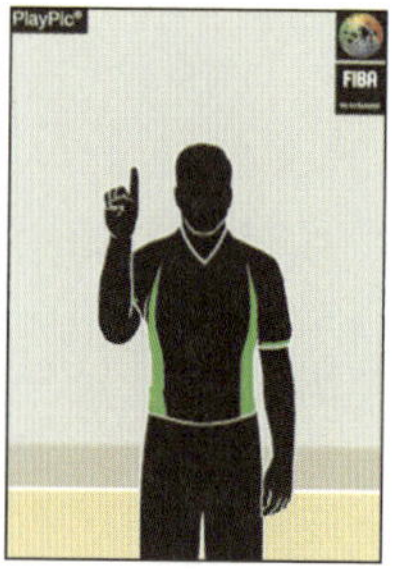

Hold up 1 finger

2 FREE THROWS

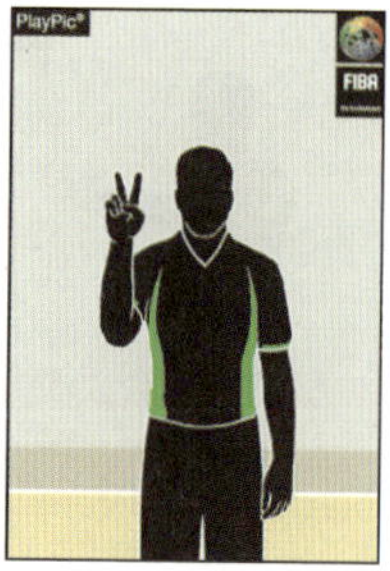

Hold up 2 fingers

3 FREE THROWS

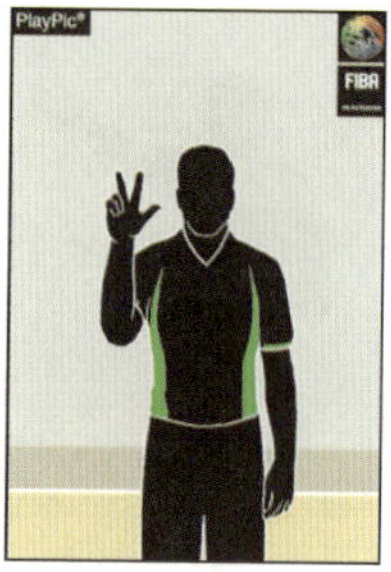

Hold up 3 fingers

向记录台报告罚则

没有罚球的犯规后

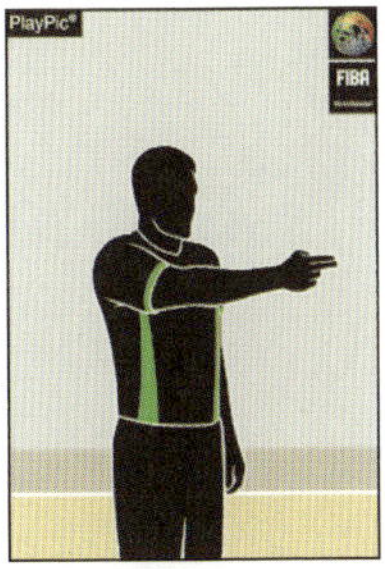

指向比赛方向，
手臂与边线平行

控制球队犯规后

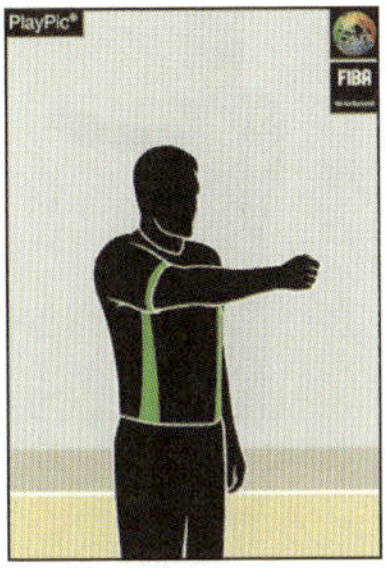

握拳指向比赛方向
手臂与边线平行

1 次罚球

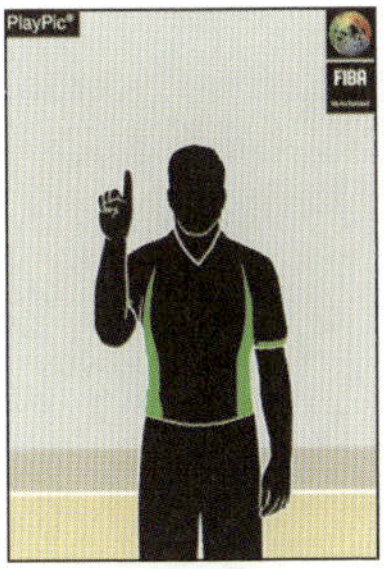

举起 1 指

2 次罚球

举起 2 指

3 次罚球

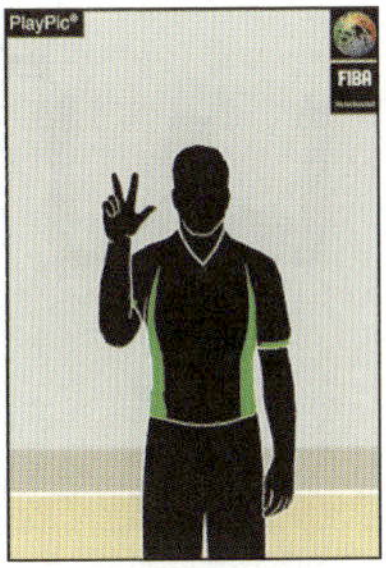

举起 3 指

Administrating Free Throws – Active Referee (Lead)

1 FREE THROW

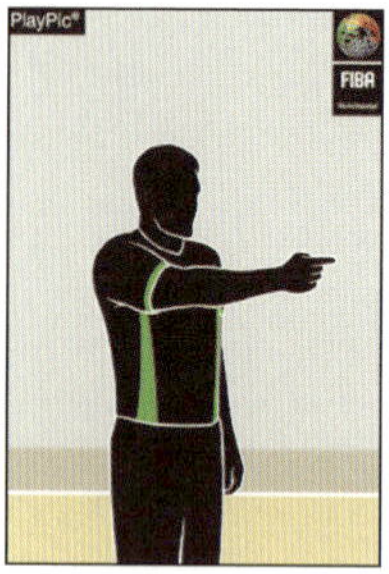

1 finger horizontal

2 FREE THROWS

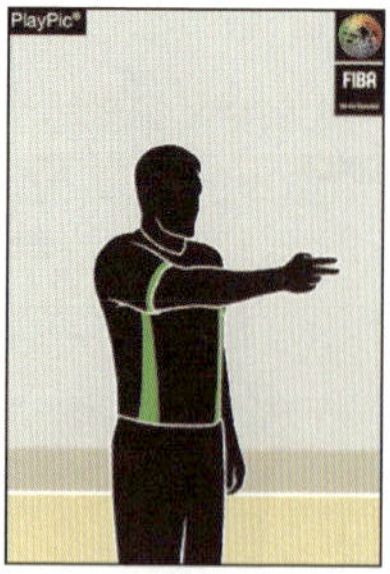

2 fingers horizontal

3 FREE THROWS

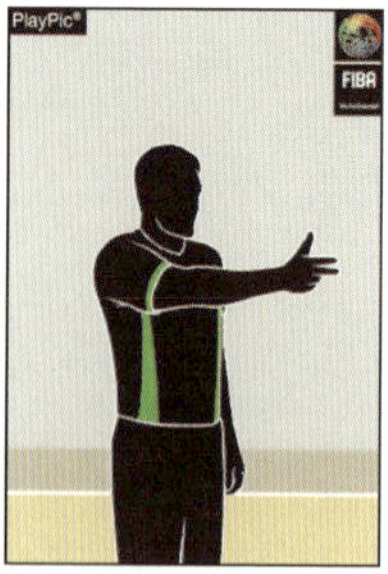

3 fingers horizontal

Administrating Free Throws – Passive Referee (Trail in 2PO & Centre in 3PO)

1 FREE THROW

Index finger

2 FREE THROWS

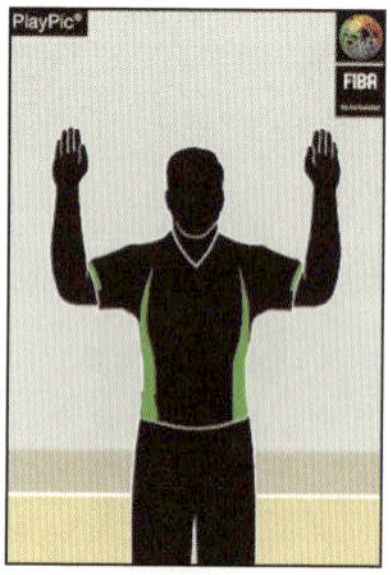

Fingers together on both hands

3 FREE THROWS

3 fingers extended on both hands

罚球管理——执行裁判（前导裁判）

1 次罚球

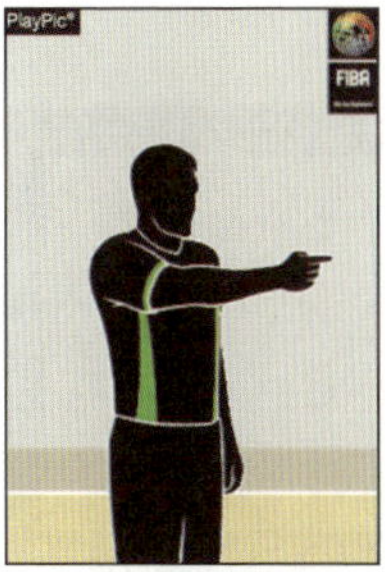

水平伸 1 指

2 次罚球

水平伸 2 指

3 次罚球

水平伸 3 指

罚球管理—非执行裁判 (2 人执裁之追踪裁判与 3 人执裁之中央裁判)

1 次罚球

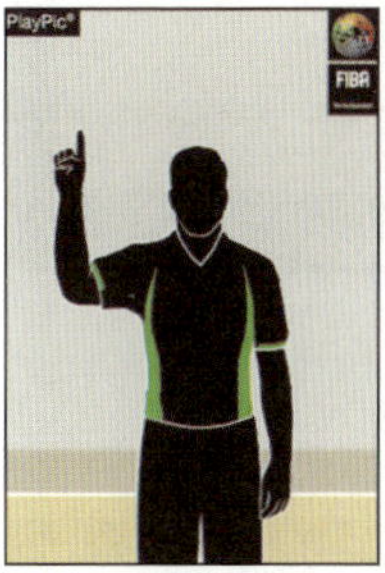

伸食指

2 次罚球

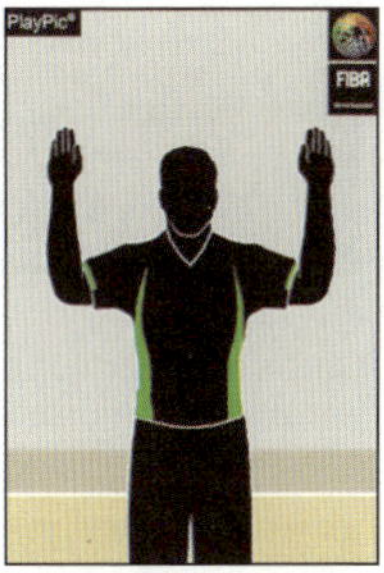

双手手指并拢

3 次罚球

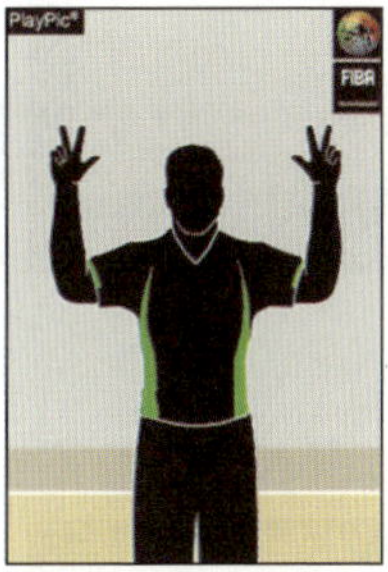

双手伸展 3 指

3.2 SWITCHES AFTER FOUL CALLS

Here is more comprehensive list of switches after foul calls.

Play remains in frontcourt, continued by throw-in

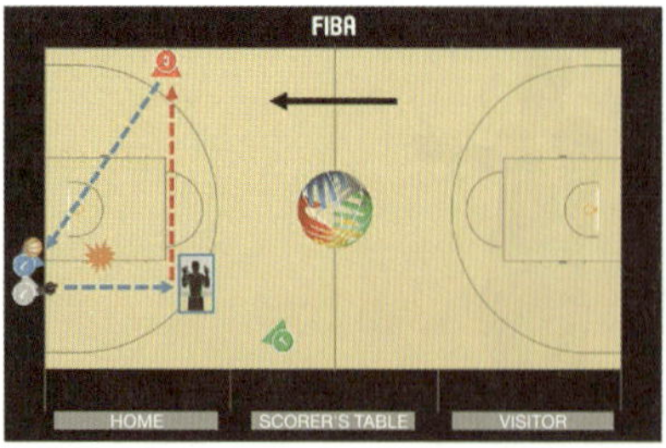

Diagramme 60:
Call frontcourt table side by L – ball remains in the frontcourt (throw-in)

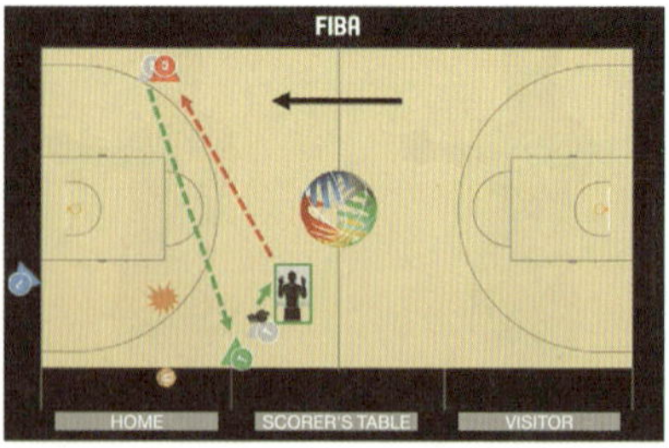

Diagram 61:
Call frontcourt table side by T – ball remains in the frontcourt (throw-in)

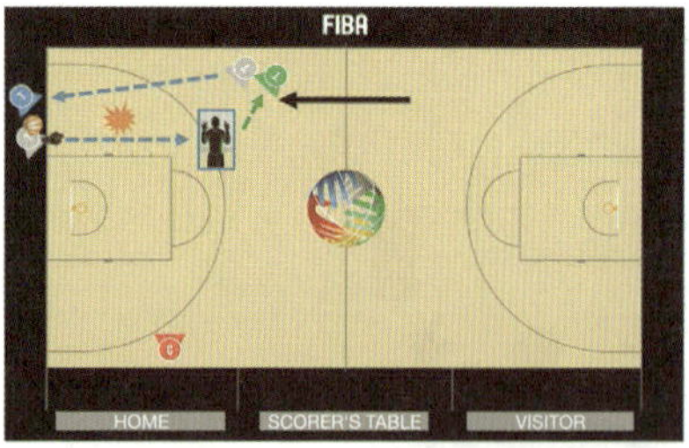

Diagram 62:
Call frontcourt opposite side by L – ball remains in the frontcourt (throw-in)

Diagram 63:
Call frontcourt opposite side by T – ball remains in the frontcourt (throw-in)

Diagram 64:
Call frontcourt table side by C – ball remains in the frontcourt (throw-in)

Diagram 65:
Call frontcourt opposite side by C – ball remains in the frontcourt (throw-in)

3.2 宣判犯规后的换位

关于宣判犯规后换位的更详细图解。

比赛仍在前场进行，掷球入界恢复比赛

图 60：
前场记录台侧，L 鸣哨——球仍位于前场（掷球入界）

图 61：
前场记录台侧，T 鸣哨——球仍位于前场（掷球入界）

图 62：
前场记录台对侧，L 鸣哨——球仍位于前场（掷球入界）

图 63：
前场记录台侧，T 鸣哨——球仍位于前场（掷球入界）

图 64：
前场记录台侧，C 鸣哨——球仍位于前场（掷球入界）

图 65：
前场记录台对侧，C 鸣哨——球仍位于前场（掷球入界）

Diagram 66:
Double call frontcourt by T & C – ball remains in the frontcourt (throw-in)

Diagram 67:
Double call frontcourt by T & C – ball remains in the frontcourt (throw-in)

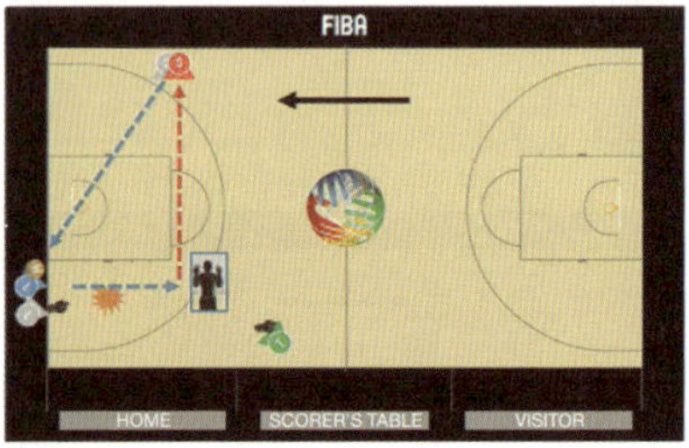

Diagram 68:
Double call frontcourt table side by T & L – ball remains in the frontcourt (throw-in)

Diagram 69:
Double call frontcourt opposite side by T & L – ball remains in the frontcourt (throw-in)

Diagram 70:
Double call frontcourt by L & C – ball remains in the frontcourt (throw-in)

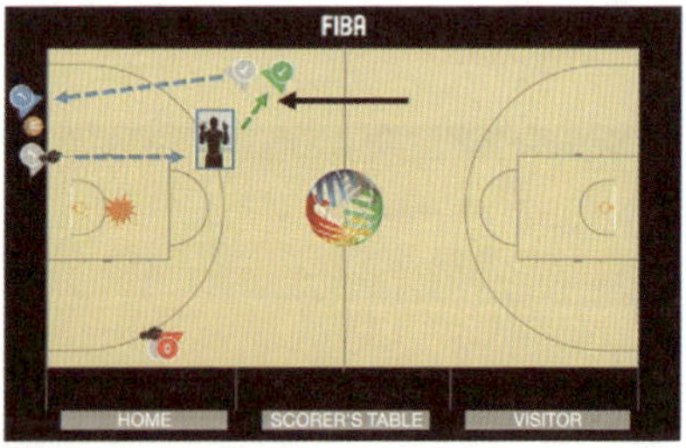

Diagram 71:
Double call frontcourt by L & C – ball remains in the frontcourt (throw-in)

图 66：
前场 T 与 C 同时鸣哨——球仍位于前场（掷球入界）

图 67：
前场 T 与 C 同时鸣哨——球仍位于前场（掷球入界）

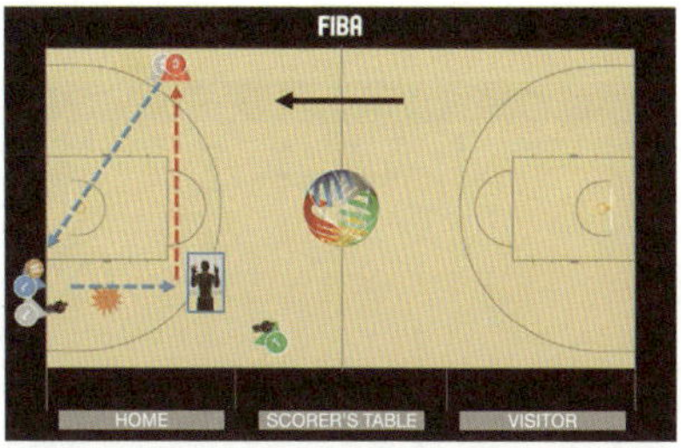

图 68：
前场记录台同侧 T 与 L 同时鸣哨——球仍位于前场（掷球入界）

图 69：
前场记录台对侧 T 与 L 同时鸣哨——球仍位于前场（掷球入界）

图 70：
前场 L 与 C 同时鸣哨——球仍位于前场（掷球入界）

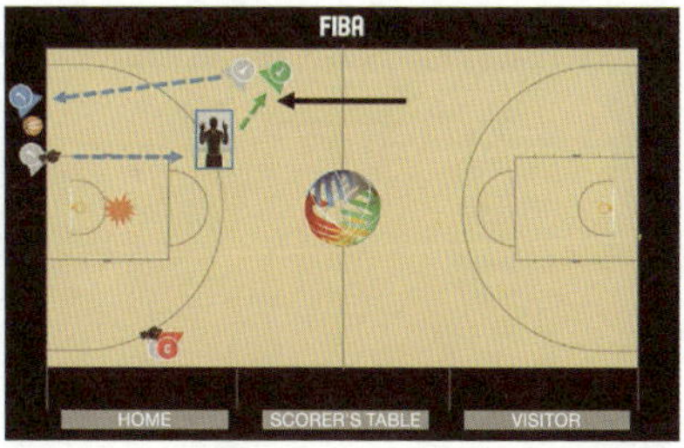

图 71：
前场 L 与 C 同时鸣哨——球仍位于前场（掷球入界）

Play remains in frontcourt, continued by free throw(s)

Diagram 72:
Call frontcourt table side by L – ball remains in the frontcourt (free throws)

Diagram 73:
Call frontcourt table side by T – ball remains in the frontcourt (free throws)

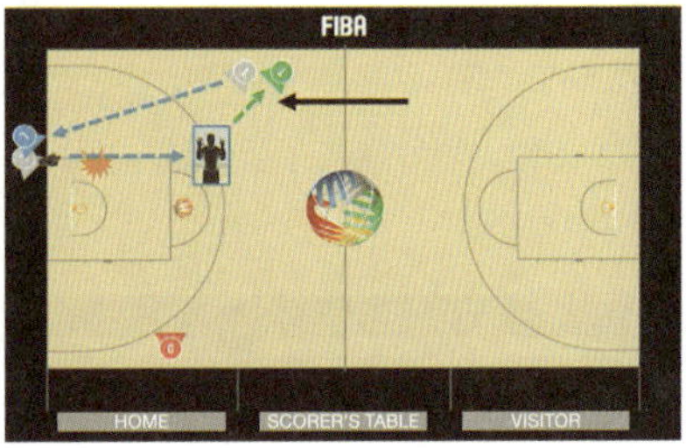

Diagram 74:
Call frontcourt opposite side by L – ball remains frontcourt (free throws)

Diagram 75:
Call frontcourt opposite side by T – ball remains in the frontcourt (free throws)

Diagram 76:
Call frontcourt table side by C – ball remains in the frontcourt (free throws)

Diagram 77:
Call frontcourt opposite side by C – ball remains in the frontcourt (free throws)

比赛仍在前场进行，罚球恢复比赛

图 72：
前场记录台同侧 L 鸣哨——球仍位于前场（罚球）

图 73：
前场记录台同侧 T 鸣哨——球仍位于前场（罚球）

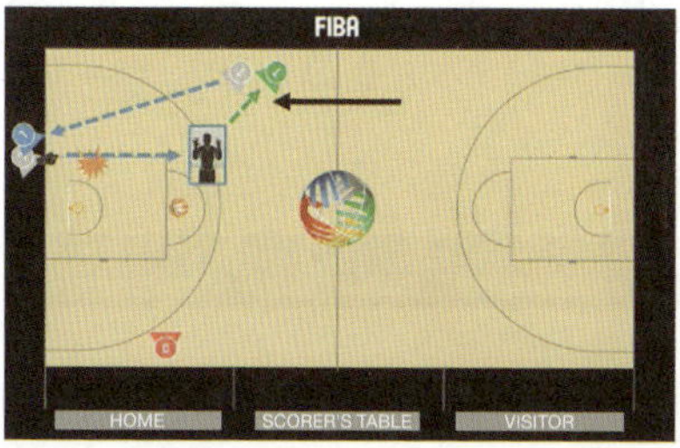

图 74：
前场记录台对侧 L 鸣哨——球仍位于前场（罚球）

图 75：
前场记录台对侧 T 鸣哨——球仍位于前场（罚球）

图 76：
前场记录台同侧 C 鸣哨——球仍位于前场（罚球）

图 77：
前场记录台对侧 C 鸣哨——球仍位于前场（罚球）

Diagram 78:
Double call frontcourt by T & C – ball remains in the frontcourt (free throws)

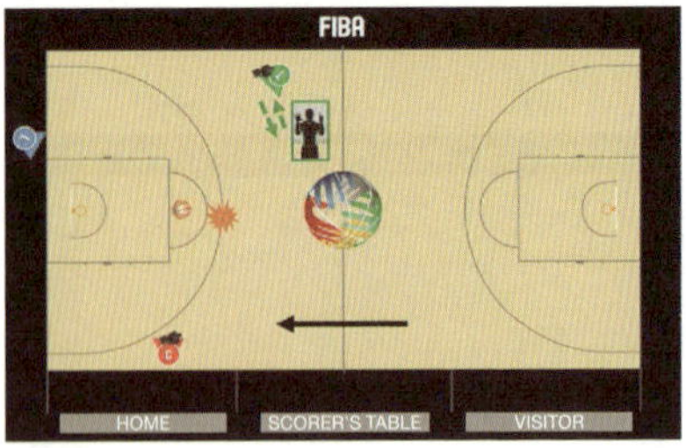

Diagram 79:
Double call frontcourt by T & C – ball remains in the frontcourt (free throws)

Diagram 80:
Double call frontcourt table side by T & L – ball remains in the frontcourt (free throws)

Diagram 81:
Double call frontcourt opposite side by T & L – ball remains in the frontcourt (free throws)

Diagram 82:
Double call frontcourt by L & C– ball remains in the frontcourt (free throws)

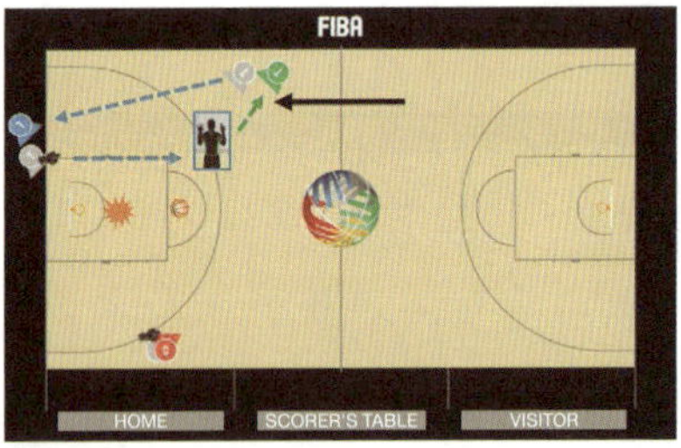

Diagram 83:
Double call frontcourt by L & C – ball remains in the frontcourt (free throws)

图 78：
前场 T 与 C 同时鸣哨——球仍位于前场（罚球）

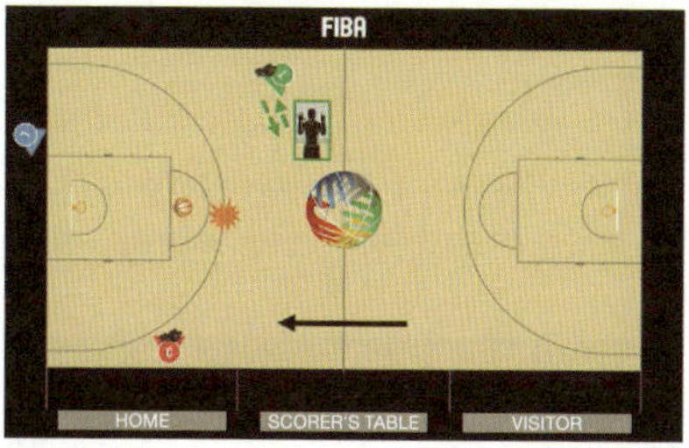

图 79：
前场 T 与 C 同时鸣哨——球仍位于前场（罚球）

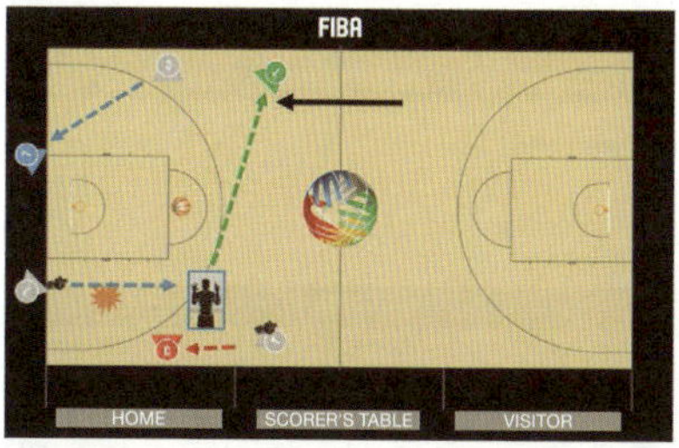

图 80：
前场记录台同侧 T 与 L 同时鸣哨——球仍位于前场（罚球）

图 81：
前场记录台对侧 T 与 L 同时鸣哨——球仍位于前场（罚球）

图 82：
前场 L 与 C 同时鸣哨——球仍位于前场（罚球）

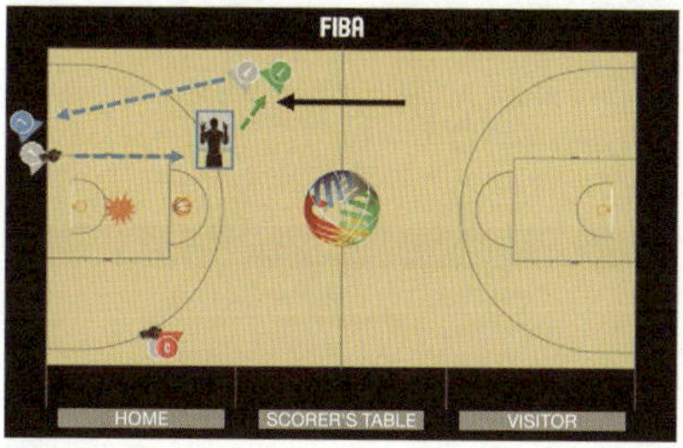

图 83：
前场 L 与 C 同时鸣哨——球仍位于前场（罚球）

Play continues from new backcourt by throw-in

Note: When a foul is called in the backcourt or there is an offensive foul in the frontcourt, there is no switch unless it is necessary to facilitate the new position of the reporting referee on the opposite side (no long switches).

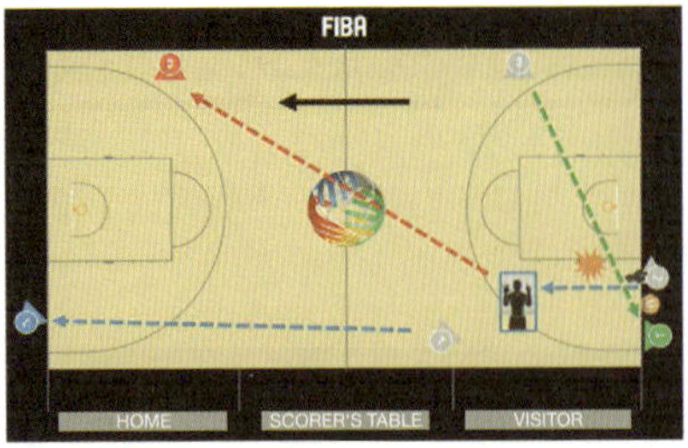

Diagram 84:
Call backcourt table side by L – ball moves new direction (throw-in)

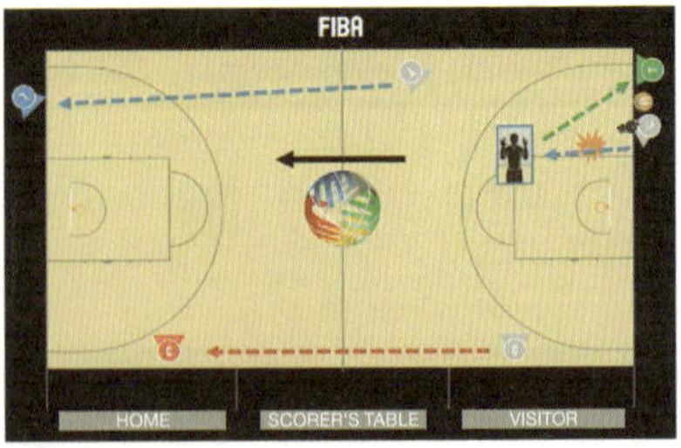

Diagram 85:
Call backcourt opposite side by L – ball moves new direction (throw-in)

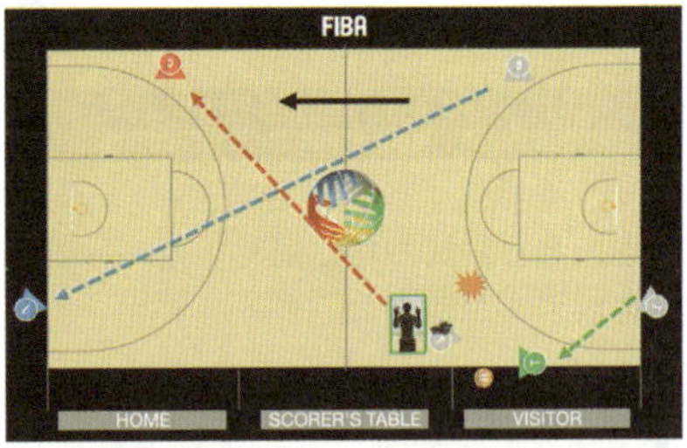

Diagram 86:
Call backcourt table side by T – ball moves new direction (throw-in)

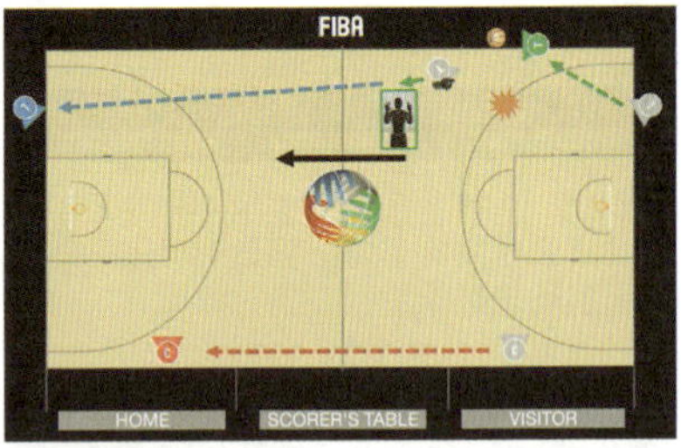

Diagram 87:
Call backcourt opposite side by T – ball moves new direction (throw-in)

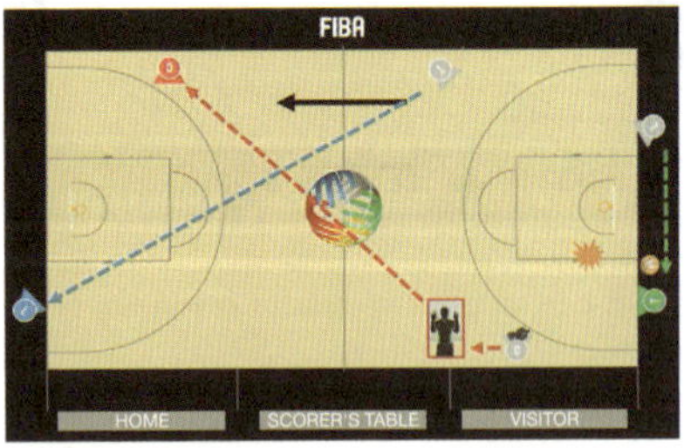

Diagram 88:
Call backcourt table side by C – ball moves new direction (throw-in)

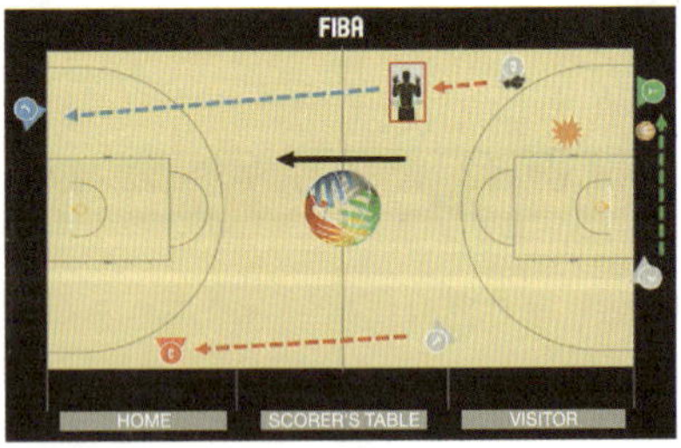

Diagram 89:
Call backcourt opposite side by C – ball moves new direction (throw-in)

比赛在新的后场继续进行

提示：当一次犯规在后场被吹罚或者在前场出现进攻犯规时，裁判员将不进行换位，除非有必要为报告裁判员在记录台对侧新位置提供便利（不要长距离换位）。

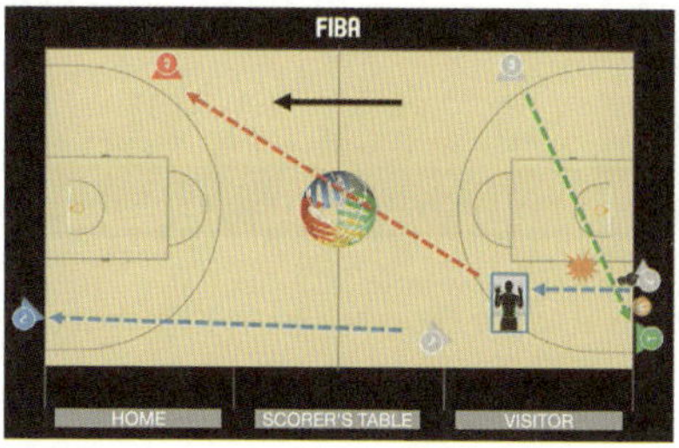

图 84：
后场记录台同侧 L 鸣哨——球向新方向移动（掷球入界）

图 85：
后场记录台对侧 L 鸣哨——球向新方向移动（掷球入界）

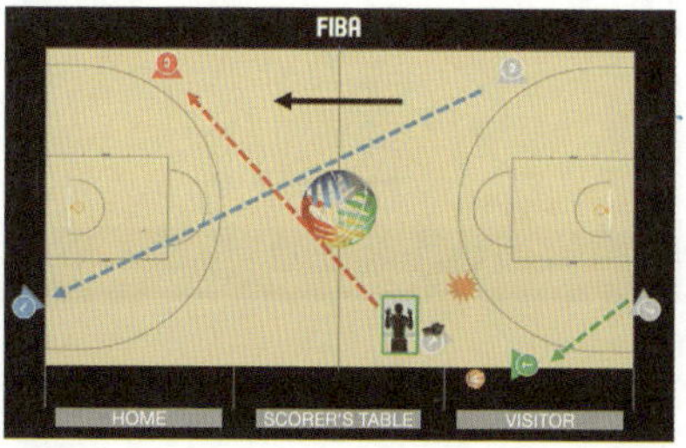

图 86：
后场记录台同侧 T 鸣哨——球向新方向移动（掷球入界）

图 87：
后场记录台对侧 T 鸣哨——球向新方向移动（掷球入界）

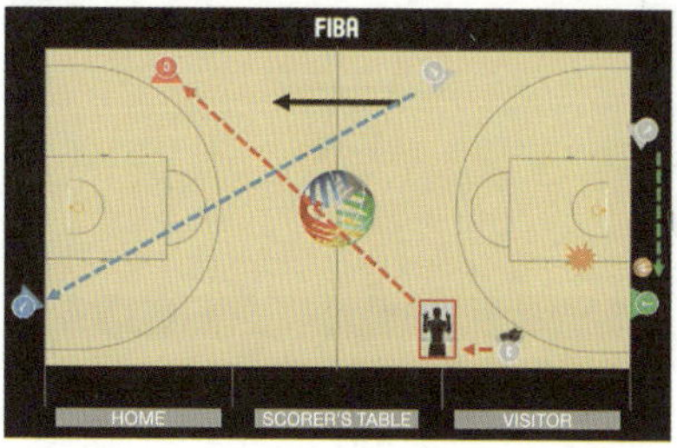

图 88：
后场记录台同侧 C 鸣哨——球向新方向移动（掷球入界）

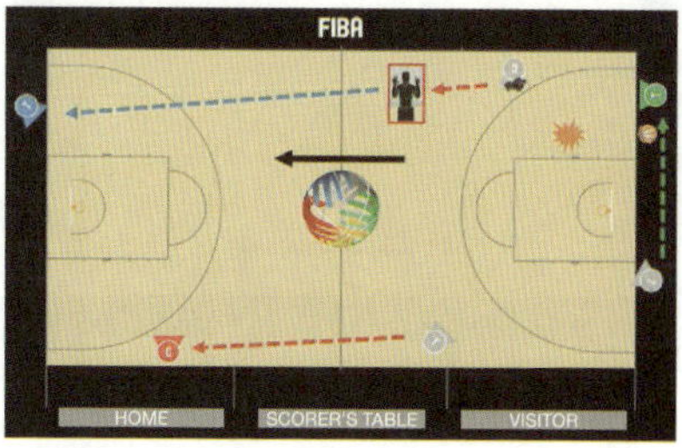

图 89：
后场记录台对侧 C 鸣哨——球向新方向移动（掷球入界）

Play continues from the opposite end of the court by free throw(s)

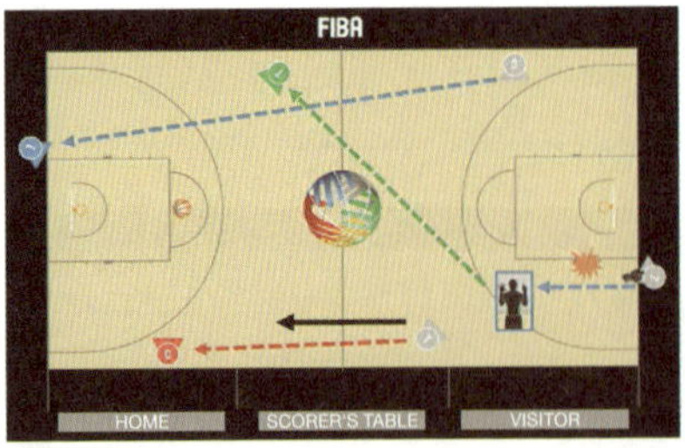

Diagram 90:
Call backcourt table side by L – ball moves new direction (free thows)

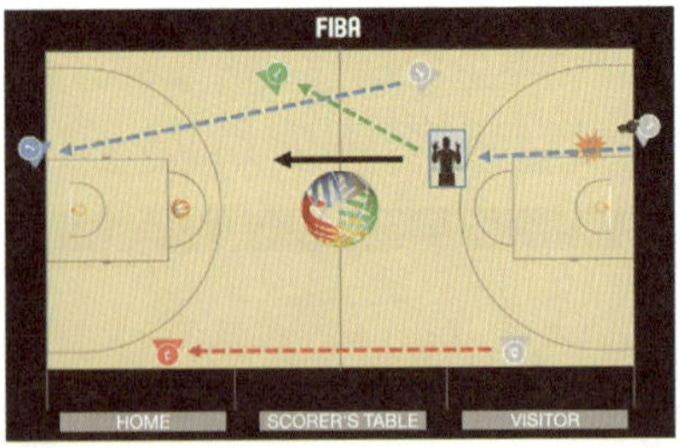

Diagram 91:
Call backcourt opposite side by L – ball moves new direction (free thows)

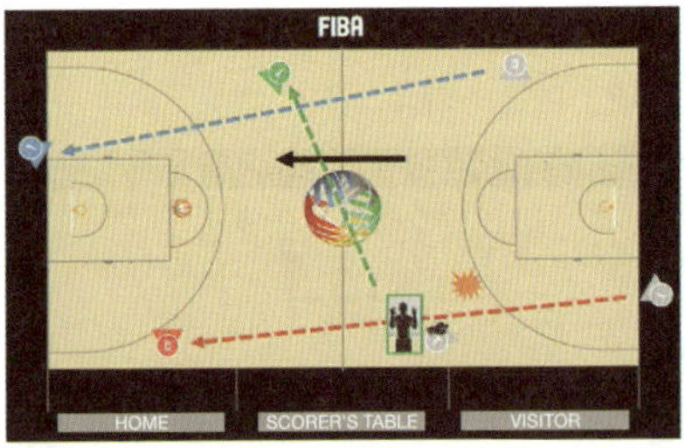

Diagram 92:
Call backcourt table side by T – ball moves new direction (free thows)

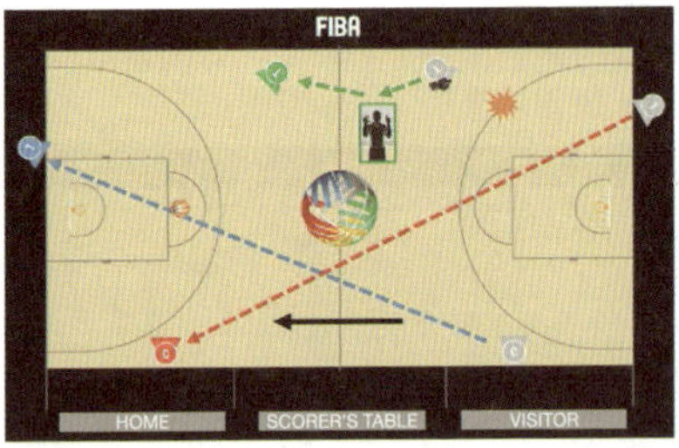

Diagram 93:
Call backcourt opposite side by T – ball moves new direction (free thows)

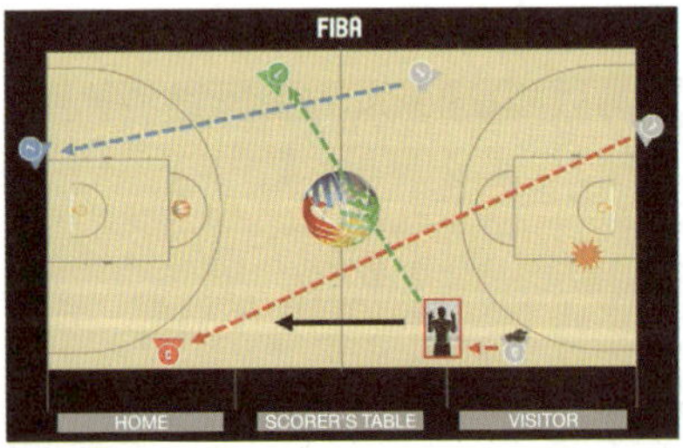

Diagram 94:
Call backcourt table side by C – ball moves new direction (free throws)

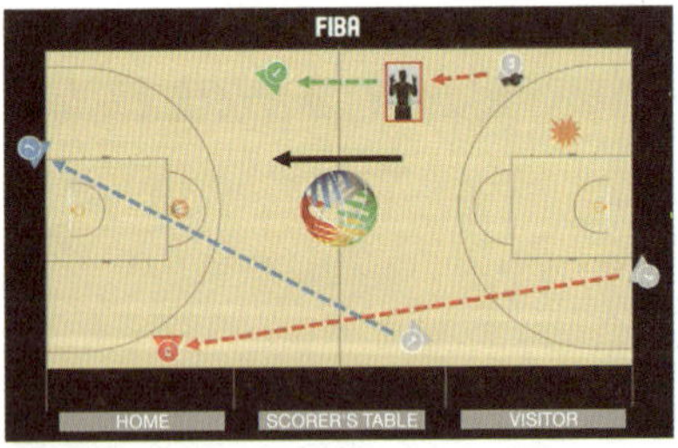

Diagram 95:
Call backcourt opposite side by C – ball moves new direction (free throws)

比赛在对面半场罚球后继续进行

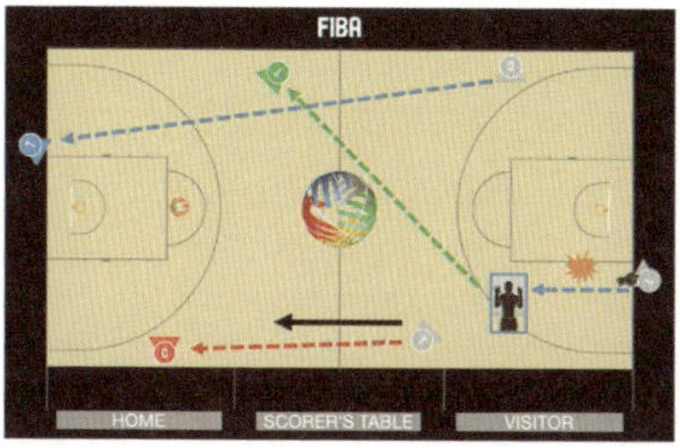

图 90：
后场记录台同侧 L 鸣哨——球向新方向移动（罚球）

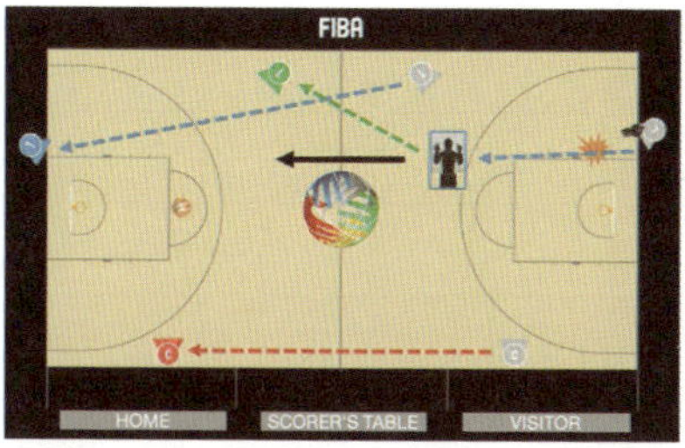

图 91：
后场记录台对侧 L 鸣哨——球向新方向移动（罚球）

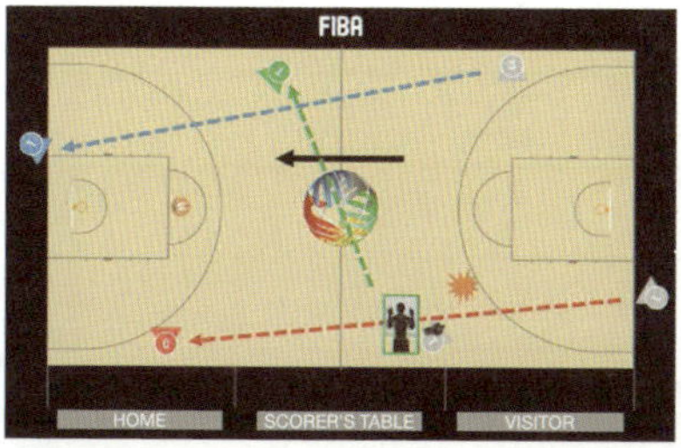

图 92：
后场记录台同侧 T 鸣哨——球向新方向移动（罚球）

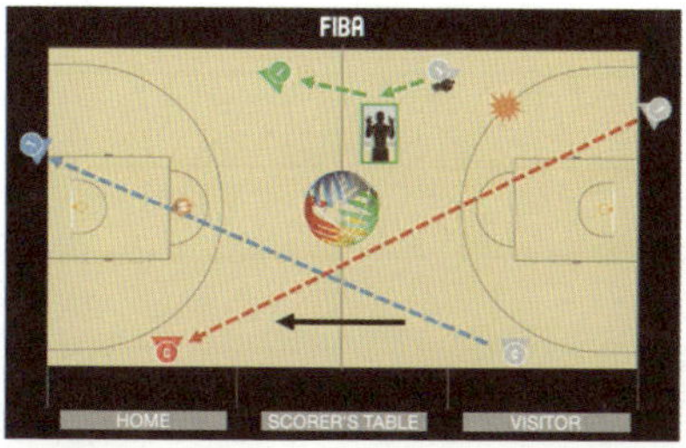

图 93：
后场记录台对侧 T 鸣哨——球向新方向移动（罚球）

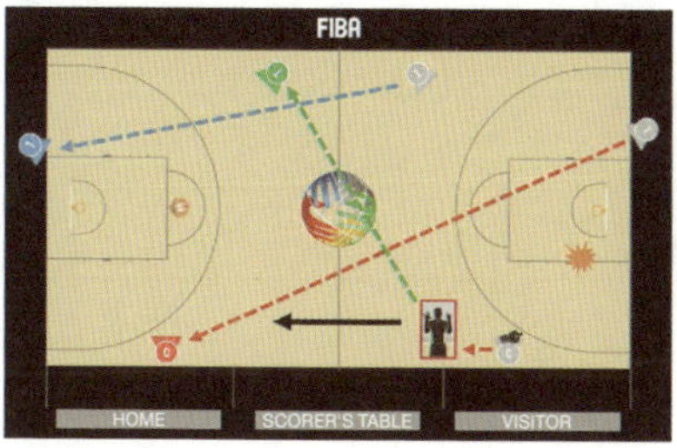

图 94：
后场记录台同侧 C 鸣哨——球向新方向移动（罚球）

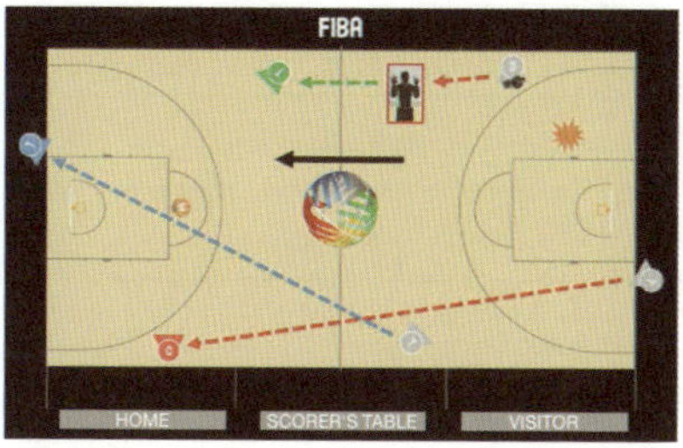

图 95：
后场记录台对侧 C 鸣哨——球向新方向移动（罚球）

NOTE

»»» NOTE

NOTE